HOSSIOS LOUKAS

PAUL LAZARIDES

Archaeologist

APOLLO EDITIONS

The following guides have been published by the APOLLO Editions and can be obtained at the corresponding archaeological sites.

Title	*By the Archaeologist*
1. Byzantine Museum of Athens. Icons	Manolis Chatzidakis
2. Byzantine Museum of Athens	Manolis Chatzidakis
3. The Minoan Civilisation and the Knossos Palace	Sonia di Neuhoff
4. The Acropolis of Athens and its Museum	M. Brouscari
5-9. From the collection of the National Museum of Athens:	
a) Bronzes	B. Kallipolitis - E. Touloupa
b) Marble masterpieces	Dimitrios Papastamos
c) Vases	Barbara Philippaki
d) Cycladic	Jianni Sakellarakis
e) Mycenaean	Petros Themelis
10. Delphi	Sonia di Neuhoff
11. Ancient Corinth and its Museum	Sonia di Neuhoff
12. Ancient Olympia	Dora Karagiorga
13. Asklipios-Epidauros and their Museum	Dimitrios Papastamos
14. Lindos	Sonia di Neuhoff
15. Hossios Loukas	Pavlos Lazarides
16. Mykonos-Delos	Petros Themelis
17. Ancient Agora	Petros Themelis
18. Sounion-Thorikos	Petros Themelis
19. Kerameikos	Petros Themelis
20. Lindos	G. Konstantinopoulos
21. Philerimos-Kamiros	G. Konstantinopoulos
22. Tyrins	J. Papachristodoulou
23. Museum of Sparta	George Steinhouer
24. Mystras	Rhodoniki Etzeoglou
25. Aegina	Sonia di Neuhoff
26. Daphni	Pavlos Lazarides
27. Brauron	Petros Themelis
28. The Necromanteion of Acheron	Sotirios Dacaris
29. Mycenae	Petros Themelis
30. The Museums of Rhodes	G. Konstantinopoulos
31. The Museum of Herakleion	M. Ioannidou
32. Knossos	M. Ioannidou

All our books are available in 8 different languages: Greek, English, Spanish, French, Italian, German, Swedish and Japanese.

Cover: *Front*: The Three Holy Infants. Mosaic. Southern drum of the cross vault.

 Back: The Temple of Hossios Loukas, from the southwest.

Text: Paul Lazarides, Archaeolog.

© E. Tzaferis, S.A. - Apollon. 52, rue Fokionos Négri. Athenes.

INDEX

FROM THE NEW BIBLIOGRAPHY
ON THE MONASTERY OF HOSSIOS LOUKAS

VEIS, N.A.: *The Monastery of Hossios Loukas the Steriotes*, volume II, 1933, page 3.

Cahiers Archéologiques: volume XIX, 1969, pages 127-150.

YANUTSOS, I.: *The byzantine temple of the monastery of Hossios Loukas over the Elikon, near Levadia, from a historic, architectural and artistic view.* Athens, 1939.

Archaeological bulletin: volume VI, 1920-1921/1923, pages 177-189.

DELVOYE, C.H.: *The byzantine monuments of Greece, in Byzance,* volume XVIII, 1946-1948, page 257.

The Byzantine art, Grenoble, 1967.

DIEZ, E., DEMENUS, O.: *Byzantine mosaics in Greece, Hossios Loukas and Daphni,* Cambridge, Massachusetts, 1931.

ACHIPRESTE JRISTOFOROS, I.: *Zone, life and narration of some miracles of Hossios Loukas,* Athens, 1937.

GRABAR: *The art by the end of the Antiquity and the Middle Age,* volume I, Paris, 1968.

MEGAW, H.: *The chronology of some byzantine churches of the Middle Age,* B.S.A., volume XXXII, 1931-1932, pages 90-130.

MORISANI, O.: *The frescoes of Hossios Loukas in Focide, Criticism of Art No. 49,* January-February, 1963.

BURAS, J.: *Byzantine cross vaults,* Athens, 1965.

ORLANDOS, A.K.: *Monastic architecture,* Athens, 1958.

STIKAS, E.: *The Chronic on the building of the Monastery of Hossios Loukas,* Athens, 1970.

G.A. SITIRIU: *Byzantine frescoes from the 11th cent. in the Crypt of Hossios Loukas in Focide,* Acts from the 3rd International Congress of Byzantine Studies, pages 389-400.

JATSIDAKIS, M.: *Byzantine monuments in Attic and Beocy,* Athens, 1956.

PROLOG

Under the influence from the moral teachings and the spirituality of the christian religion, by the beginning of the first centuries, and specially during the 3rd century of our time, lots of people left the towns and the world looking for shelter in recondite places where they continiously praye and read the Holy Scriptures and spent a real ascetic life.

People were highly impressed by these ascetics. For this reason, and during the next century, i. e. 4th century, a great number of people went to the deserts of Egypt, Syria and Minor Asia, places of habitat of these ascetics, in order to join them and to found monasteries. Basilius the Great was the first to impose the rules which would lead the monastic life.

From the information that we have received and mostly from the foundings made out during the archaeological excavations, one may assume that in Greece monasteries started to be built at least in the 5th century of our time, for instance in Daphni, Cesarini, Pargas from Megara, etc.

Some of these men, wanting to lead a real hard ascetic life, settled down in places very difficult to reach, for exemple in caves, etc., where they lived in a completely ascetic way. These ascetics called «asketerioi» are spread in several places of the country, Himetos, Parnes, Pentelikon, Agia Larisis, Etoloacarnania, Euritania, etc. In the 8th century, during the salvage incursions from the pagans, the monasteries were abandoned. From and after the 10th century, however, the monastic life experiments a new impulse. In all places, monasteries were built.

The most important are: The monastery of Hossios Loukas (10th century); the monastery of the Philosopher, near Dimitsana, in Gortinia (founded under the kingdom of Nikiforos Fokas, 963-961 after Christ); the monastery of Varnakova, in Dorida; the monastery of Sagmata, near Thebes; the monastery of Skafidias, near Amaliada; the monastery of Kukus, near Astros Kinurias; the monastery of Agios Georgios, near Egion; the monastery of Hossios Meletios in Kicerona, and many others.

These monasteries played a very important part during the uneasy times that lived the orthodox church and the nation. The protectors defended sometimes with stubbornness and fanaticism, the orthodox faith. These were the centers of the letters, the arts and the sciences. Everybody knows that, in the past, the monasteries constituted the only public libraries and the only places where the Greec letters were cultivated, transcribing the works of the Sciences and Wisdom and forwarding them to our time.

To the activity of the monasteries owe their origin the Occult Schools of the People enslaved during the Turkish dominion.

The humanitary mission was one of the most important aims of the Monasteries. The monks, following the exemple of Basilius the Great, cure the ills, look after the poors, offer hospitality to the pilgrims and shelter under their roof the miserables and the unfortunates.

The presence of the monasteries was also of importance during the flourishing of the nation. They were the centers, the bastions and the splendour of the hellenism. Undoubtedly, the monasteries contributed in a big way to the independence of Greece. The monasteries of Hossios Loukas, Agia Lavra, Mega Spileon and hundreds of them will show forever the steps followed by the history of the hellenistic nation.

CLASSIFICATION OF ICONOGRAPHIC AND DECORATIVE THEMES IN THE NAVE, CHURCH OF THE VIRGIN AND CRYPT

Below we describe all the compositions and iconographic themes, representations, individual figures of saints, temples, etc. that visitors can see nowadays. We are not going to mention the places closed to visitors.

The classification is as follows:

I. CHURCH OF HOSSIOS LOUKAS (Nave)

1. NARTHEX:

    A.   Central space and cross vault.
    B.   Left Northern space and cross vault.
    C.   Right Southern space and cross vault.

2. MAIN TEMPLE:

    D.   Space just after the door.
    E.   Southerly cross vault, to the right.
    F.   Southeast Chapel.
    G.   Northerly cross vault, to the left.
    H.   Northeast Chapel.
    I.   Dome.
    J.   Northeast squinch and surfaces of the walls that meet under it.
    K.   Southwest squinch and surfaces of the walls that meet under it.
    L.   Northeast squinch and surfaces of the walls that meet under it.
    M.   Western Chamber of the cross of ceiling, up over space *D.*
    N.   South Chamber of the cross of ceiling, up over space...
    O.   Space to the South of the door to the ground floor, cross vault, floor.

P. Septentrional Chamber of the cross of ceiling,
    up over space Q.
Q. Space to the North of the door to the ground floor,
    cross vault, walls, reliquary, floor.

3. HOLY PULPIT:
R. Temple. Iconostasis.
S. Main Sanctuary, stories, side walls, floor.
T. Prosthesis, North from Main Sanctuary.
U. Diaconicon, South from Main Sanctuary.

II. CHURCH OF THE VIRGIN

A. Temple. Iconostasis, floor.
B. Arched opening between Sanctuary and Diaconicon.
C. Diaconicon.

III. CRIPT

A. Chamber just after the entrance.
B. Space just after the cross vault A.
C. Southeast angular space with low vault (CA-
    LOTTE).
D. North from C. It is the first place of the main space
    from western.
E. Northeast angular space.
F. East from the latter, septentrional space where the
    Tomb of Hossios Loukas lies.
G. South from the latter, cross vault between F and B.
H. Northeast angular space.
I. South from the latter, cross vault between H and A.
J. Southeast angular space.
K. Eastern cross vault that covers the Sanctuary.

IV. OUTSIDE VIEWS OF THE BUILDINGS

V. PLANS

As one can see on the plans, the space between the two temples and the crypt, thanks to the various elements of construction and architecture, are divided into several departments. For this reason, the classification of the themes according to each of the departments was necessary and useful, first of all, in order that the visitor can follow the way which will unable him, without difficulty, to go through all the places of the temples, and secondly, in order that he can recognise and comprehend all that he sees.

CLASSIFICATION OF ICONOGRAPHIC AND DECORATIVE THEMES

Here are classified the iconographic themes, compositions, individuals, mosaics, frescoes, icons, sculptures, etc. in accordance with the classification below mentioned. First of all, the themes concerning the main temple (the Nave), afterwards, the Church of the Virgin, and finally the Crypt, following by correlative order the Narthex, the Main Temple, the Sanctuary, etc., as well as the various departments and spaces. The numeration of the themes is made by correlative order for each temple, i. e., it is different for the Main Temple, for the Church of the Virgin and also for the Crypt.

Looking at the catalogue we shall see the following characteristics: the roman numbers I, II, III, IV and V show the three temples, the outside views and the plans; *a*, *b*, *c*, show the three parts of the Nave, Narthex, Main Temple and the Holy Pulpit; *A*, *B*, *C*, *D*, etc., the departments of each temple; 1, 2, 3, 4, etc. the numeration of themes in each temple, etc., the description or title of the themes. Finally, on the right side of the page, the words «Paintings» and the correlative numbers from 1 to 42 correspond to the colour plates in the present catalogue. The descriptions, titles and descriptions of the themes are written in greek, according to ortographical order.

I. CHURCH OF HOSSIOS LOUKAS (Nave)

a) NARTHEX:.

A. Cross vault central space.

    1. Christ as Master.   Painting 1
Drum of the arch over the door
to the Temple.

    2. Me(ter) C(eo)u. Virgin   Painting 2
Cross vault.

    3. IE Arj(ággelos) Gabriel.   Painting 2

    4. A(gios) Io(annis) o   Painting 2
(Pró)dr (omos). Cross vault.

    5. Arj(ággelos) Mij(ail).   Painting 2
Cross vault.

    6. A(gios) Anembódistos.
Arch over the western entrance.

    7. Agios Pigasios.
Arch over the western entrance.

    8. Agios Akíndinos.
Arch over the western entrance.

    9. Agios Afzonios.
Arch over the western entrance.

   10. A(gios) Elpidiforos.
Arch over the western entrance.

   11. Agios Petros.
Eastern part of the arch, North
from Christ.

   12. Agios Marcos.
In the center of the same arch.

   13. Agios Andreas.
Western part of the same arch.

B. Septentrional space to the left and cross vault.

   14. The Crucifixion.   Painting 3
Drum of the Eastern arch.

   15. Agios Cosmás. Cross vault.

   16. Agios Kiros.

   17. Agios Damianós (ruined).
Cross vault.

18. A(gios) Io(annis).
Cross vault.

19. A(gios) Matheos.   Painting 4
Eastern part of the septentrional
arch.

20. Agios Simón.   Painting 4
In the middle of the same arch.

21. A(gios) Lucás.   Painting 4
Western part of the same arch.

22. Baptismal Font.   Painting 4
Niche of northern wall.

23. Agia Irene.   Painting 5
Drum of western arch.

24. Agia Ekaterina.   Painting 5
Drum of western arch.

25. Agia Barbara.   Painting 5
Drum of western arch.

26. Agia Eufemia.   Painting 5
Drum of western arch.

27. Agia Marina.   Painting 5
Drum of western arch.

28. Agia Iuliane.   Painting 5
Drum of western arch.

C. Southern space to the right and cross vault.

29. Agios Paulos.   Painting 6
Eastern part of the arch between
A and C.

30. Agios Iácobos.
In the middle of the same arch.

31. Agios Io(annis) the Theologian.
Western part of the arch between
A and C.

32. Anástasis (Resurrection), or the   Painting 7
Descension to Hades.
Drum of eastern arch.

33. A(gios) Thomás.   Painting 8
Eastern part of southern arch.

34. A(gios) Barzolomeos.   Painting 8
In the middle of the same arch.

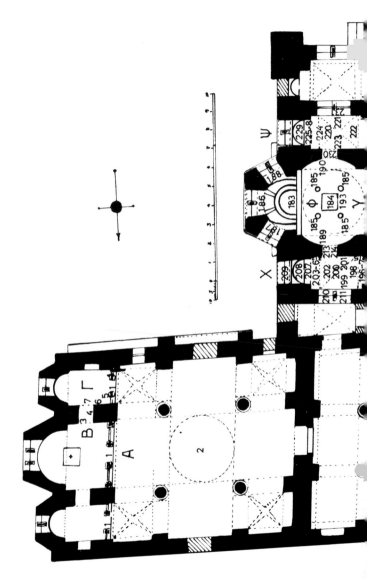

II

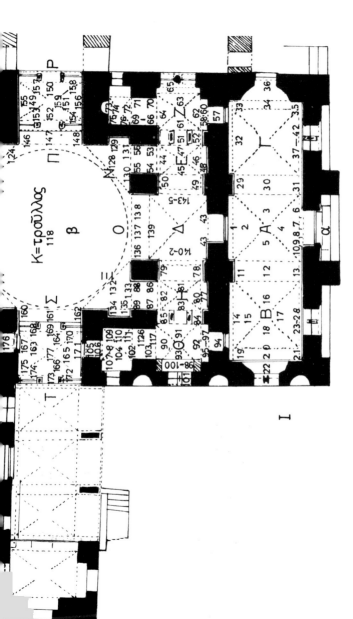

35.	A(gios) Filipos.	Painting 8
	Western part of the same arch.	
36.	Closed door. (The incredulity of Thomas.)	Painting 8
	Niche in southern wall.	
37.	Agia Cekla.	Painting 9
	Drum of western arch.	
38.	Saints Constantine and Helen.	Painting 9
	Drum of western arch.	
39.	Agia Agaci.	Painting 9
	Drum of western arch.	
40.	Agia An(a)stasía.	Painting 9
	Drum of western arch.	
41.	Agia Febronía.	Painting 9
	Drum of western arch.	
42.	Agia Eugenía.	Painting 9
	Drum of western arch.	

b) MAIN TEMPLE:

D. Central cross vault just after door.

43. Epigraph of Monk Gregory in two parts to the left and to the right of the door.

E. Southeasterly cross vault between *A* and *F*.

44.	Agios Pimin. Cross vault.	Painting 10
45.	A(gios) Io(annis) the Kalivitis. Cross vault.	Painting 10
46.	Agios Abramios. Cross vault.	Painting 10
47.	A(gios) Io(annis) the Kolovós. Cross vault.	Painting 10
48.	A(gios) Nikon the Metanoite. Western wall.	Painting 10
49.	A(gios) Makarios the Egyptien. Northern arch.	Painting 10
50.	A(gios) Io(annis) the one from the Climax. Northern arch.	Painting 10
51.	Agios Stéfanos, the Young. Drum of aperture of three arches.	Painting 10

52.	Agios Martinianós. Drum of aperture of three arches.	Painting 10
53.	Agios Sabas. Eastern arch.	Painting 10
54.	Agios Pajomios. Eastern arch.	Painting 10
55.	Agios Efcimios. Eastern arch.	Painting 10
56.	Agios Ceodosios. Eastern arch.	Painting 10

F. Southwesterly Chapel (Frescoes).

57.	The three Saints. There is only one preserved in the drum of the arch on the western wall.	
58.	Agios Akakios. Western wall over arched door.	
59.	Agios Ioannis the Kolovós. Western part over arched door.	
60.	Agios. Western wall over arched door.	
61.	Martyr, bust on cross vault.	Painting 11
62.	Martyr, bust on cross vault.	Painting 11
63.	Martyr, bust on cross vault.	Painting 11
64.	Martyr, bust on cross vault.	Painting 11
65.	Model of church. Southern window with two arches.	Painting 11
66.	Agios Dimitrios. Northern wall.	Painting 11
67.	Agios Sergios. Northern wall.	Painting 11
68.	Agios Nikitas. Northern wall.	Painting 11
69.	Agios Bacos. Northern wall.	Painting 11
70.	Agios Nestor. In front of Saint Dimitrios.	Painting 11
71.	Agios Ignatios. Below Saint Dimitrios.	Painting 11
72.	Cross and blessing hand. Eastern vault.	Painting 11
73.	Virgin and Child. Niche.	Painting 12
74.	Agios Azanasios. North from the Virgin.	Painting 12

75.	Walking Christ.	Painting 13
	Eastern wall. Epigraph.	
76.	Agios Ioannis Prodromos.	Painting 13
	Epigraph. Northern wall.	

Northwesterly cross vault between *D* and *H* (Mosaics).

77.	A(gios) Likás the Gurnikiotis.	Painting 14
	Western wall.	
78.	A(gios) Daniel. Southern arch.	Painting 14
79.	A(gios) Ceodoros the Studitis.	Painting 14
80.	Agios Ceoktistos. Cross vault.	Painting 14
81.	Agios Doroceos. Cross vault.	Painting 14
82.	Agios Nilos. Cross vault.	Painting 14
83.	Agios Máximos. Cross vault.	Painting 14
84.	Agios Ioanikios.	Painting 14
	Drum of the three northern arches.	
85.	Agios Sisiois.	Painting 14
	Drum of the three northern arches.	
86.	Agios Hilarion. Eastern arch.	Painting 14
87.	Agios Arsenios. Eastern arch.	Painting 14
88.	Agios Efraim. Eastern arch.	Painting 14
89.	Agios Antonios. Eastern arch.	Painting 14

H. Northwesterly Chapel (frescoes).

90.	Agios Agapios.
	Eastern cross vault.
91.	Agios Efstasios.
	Eastern cross vault.
92.	Agios Ceopistos.
	Eastern cross vault.
93.	Agios (?). Eastern cross vault.
94.	The Ascension of Prophet Ilios.
	On the top of western wall.
95.	Christ Emmanuel.
	Below Ilios.
96.	Agia Barbara. Below Ilios.

97. Prophet Iliseos. Below Ilios.
98. Agios Nikiforos (?).
    Northern wall.
99. Agios Cristóforos.
    Northern wall.
100. Agios (?). Northern wall.
101. Tomb. Northern wall (below).
102. Archangel Mijail (?).
    Northern part of arch.
103. Agios Ceodoros (?).
    Below the Archangel.
104. The Pantocrator.
    In the low eastern vault.
105. The Transfiguration.
    Eastern wall.
106. Agios Lukás. Eastern wall.
107. Agia Iuliti.
    Eastern wall. Left.
108. Agios Kírikos.
    Eastern wall. Left.
109. Agios (?). Eastern wall. Right.
110. Agios (?). Eastern wall. Right.
111. The Crucifixion.
    Southern wall, above.
112-116. The five Saints.   Painting 15
117. The Archangel Gabriel (?).
    Southern part of arch.

I.   Dome (Frescoes).

   118. The Pantocrator, the Virgin, the   Painting 16
        Prodromos, four Archangels and
        16 Prophets.

J.   Northeasterly squinch and the low surfaces of the
       walls (mosaics).

   119. The Evangelicism.
        Northeasterly squinch (ruined).
   120. Agios Vasilios.   Painting 17
        Niche of Northern wall.

K. Southeasterly squinch and the low surfaces of the walls.

121. The Nativity. Mosaic.   Painting 18
122. Agios Afxendios. Left from Nativity. Mosaic.
123-124. Agios Fikentios and Agios Viktor. Right from Nativity. Frescoes (loose).
125. The Virgin, at the eastern aperture of two arches, below the Nativity. Mosaic.
126. Agia Ana, at the southern aperture of two arches. Mosaic.
127. A(gios) Io(annis) or Jri(sosto)mos. Niche of Southern wall below the Nativitý. Mosaic.   Painting 19

L. Southwesterly squinch and the low surfaces of the walls.

128. Ypapantí.   Painting 20
129. Agios Adrianos. At the southern aperture of two arches below Ypapantí.
130. Agios Trifon. At the western aperture of two arches.
131. Agios Nikolaos. Niche of southern wall below Ypapantí.

M. Squinch and the low surfaces of the wall (mosaics).

132. The Baptism.   Painting 21
133. Agios Agazángelos. Western aperture of two arches.
134. Agios. Northern aperture of two arches.
135. Agios Grigorios the Thaumaturgus. Niche of northern wall below the Baptism.

N. Western Chamber of the cross of the roof, above over *D*.

136. Agios Mercurios.
Northern middle of eastern arch.
137. Agios Cristof(o)ros. Mosaic.
About the middle of the arch.
138. Agios Prokopios. Mosaic.
Southern middle of arch
139. Agios Simon. Mosaic.
There is only a part left.
140-142. The three Saints.
Frescoes on the northern aperture of three arches.
143-144. The three Saints.
Frescoes on the southern aperture of three arches.

O Southern chamber of the cross of the roof, above, over *P* (mosaics).

146. Agios Zeodoros the Tiron.
Eastern halfarch.
147. Agios Nestor.
In the middle of the arch.
148. Agios Dimitrios.
Western halfarch.

P. Cross vault of the southern door to the ground floor (mosaics).

149. I(isus) X(ristós). Christ.	Painting 22
150. Archangel Uriel.	Painting 22
151. Agios Zajarias.	Painting 22
152. Archangel Raphael.	Painting 22
153. Agios Kleopas.	Painting 22
Northern aperture of three arches.	
154. Agios Ananias.	Painting 22
Northern aperture of three arches.	

155. The Panagia (Virgin).   Painting 22
     On the eastern wall.
156. Agios Panteleimon.   Painting 22
     On the western wall.
157. Agios Sosípatros.   Painting 22
     On the southern window.
158. Agios Iason.   Painting 22
     On the southern window.
159. Marble plate, on the floor.

Q. Northern chamber of the cross of the roof, above,
    over R.

160. Agios Georgios. Mosaic.
     To the middle from the arch of
     the temple.
161. Agios Nikolaos the Young.
     Fresco in the middle of the same
     arch (loose).
162. Agios Zeodoros the Stratilatis.
     Fresco in the same arch (loose).

R. Cross vault of northern door to ground floor.

163. I(isus) X(ristós).
     Mosaic. Cross vault.
164. The Archangel Mikael.
     Mosaic. Cross vault.
165. A(gios) Iakobos the Adelfoceos.
     (Brother of God).
     Mosaic. Cross vault.
166. The Archangel Gabriel.
     Mosaic Cross vault.
168. Agios Silas. Mosaic. Southern
     aperture of three arches.
169. Agios Timoceos. Mosaic.
     Southern aperture of three ar-
     ches.
170. Agios Nikanor. Mosaic.
     Southern aperture of three ar-
     ches.

171. Agios Lukás. Mosaic.   Painting 23
     Western wall.
172. Agios Barnabas. Mosaic.
     Northern aperture of thrée ar-
     ches.
173. Agios Stéfanos the Protomartyr.
     Mosaic. Northern aperture of
     three arches.
174. Agios Prójoros. Mosaic.
     Northern aperture of three ar-
     ches.
175. I(isus) from Naví. Fresco.   Painting 24
     Eastern wall below the Virgin.
176. Marble «Proskinitarion» and re-
     liquary.
     Eastern wall below the Virgin.
177. Marble plate on the floor.

c) HOLY PULPIT.

S. 178. Marble Iconostasis.   Painting 25
    179. «Panton Elpís».   Painting 25
         Portable icon of the Virgin of the
         Passion.
    180. The «Pantocrator».   Painting 25
         Portable icon of Christ.
    181. «Agios Ioanis o Prodromos».
         Portable icon on the southern
         wall below Agios Ioannis the Jri-
         sóstomos.
    182. «Agios Lukás the Stirios of Hel-
         las». Portable icon on the
         northern wall below Agios Ba-
         silios.

T. 183. The «Platitera».   Painting 26
         Epigraph, mosaic. Niche.
    184. Whitsuntide.
         Mosaic. Vault of the sanctuary.
    185. Races, languages about Whit-
         suntide.

186. Christ. Mosaic between the central aperture of two arches from the niche window, below the Virgin.
187. The Virgin. Mosaic in the aperture of the northern window of two arches.
188. Agios Ioannis the Prodromos. Mosaic in the aperture of the southern window of two arches.
189. Agios Grigorios the Theologian. Mosaic, in the northern niche of rather small deepness.
190. Agios Azanasios. Mosaic. In the southern niche of rather small deepness.
191. The Archangel Mikael. Mosaic on the arch.
192. The Archangel Gabriel. Mosaic on the arch.
193. Marble plate on the floor.   Painting 27

U. «Prótesis» (Left from the Pulpit)

194. A(gios) Kirilos of Alexandria. Mosaic. Arch over the Temple.
195. A(gios) Klimis (Pope of Rome?). Mosaic. Arch over the Temple.
196. A(gios) Ignatios the Theoforos. Mosaic. Arch over the Temple.
197. A(gios) Grigorios of Great Armenia. Mosaic. Arch over the Temple.
198. A(gios) Mijail. Fresco in the cross vault.
199. (Agios) Leonidas. Fresco in the cross vault.
200. Agios Parc(enios). Fresco in the cross vault.
202. (Agios) Babilas. Fresco in the cross vault.

202. Epigraph.
     Mosaic. Arch of niche.
203-206. Four Angels.
     Fresco. Arch of niche.
207. The Holy Spirit.
     Fresco. Arch of niche.
208. «Paleos ton imerón».
     Fresco. Niche.
209. «Akra Tapínosis». (Humiliation).
     Christ Ceotokos, John the Theo-
     logian. Fresco, niche below the
     aperture of the two arched win-
     dow.
210. Agios Basilios.
     Fresco. Northern wall.
211. Agios Grigorios the Theologian.
     Fresco. Northern wall.
212. Agios Ioannis Jrisóstomos.
     Fresco. Southern wall.
213. Agios Azanasios.
     Fresco. Southern wall.
214. Agios Sergios and Agios Bacos.
     Fresco. Southern drum of the
     cross vault.
215. Epigraph, fresco. Southern wall.

d) DIAKONIKON (right from the Pulpit).

216. Agios Dionisios Areopagitis.   Painting 28
     Mosaic. Western arch.
217. Agios Hieroceos.   Painting 28
     Mosaic. Western arch.
218. Agios Grigorios Nisis.   Painting 28
     Mosaic. Western arch.
219. Agios Filoceos.   Painting 28
     Mosaic. Western arch.
220. Agios Antipas.   Painting 28
     Mosaic. Cross vault.
221. Agios Elfecerios.   Painting 28
     Mosaic. Cross vault.

23

222. Agios Ancimos.   Painting 28
     Mosaic. Cross vault.
223. Agios Policarpos.   Painting 28
     Mosaic. Cross vault.
224. Epigraph.   Painting 28
     Mosaic. Arch of niche.
225. Agios Agilios. Mosaic. Niche.
226. Agios Kiprianós. Mosaic. Niche.
227. Agios Spiridon. Mosaic. Niche.
228. Agios Silvestros. Mosaic. Niche.
229. Agios Ceodoros from Tiron.
     Mosaic. Niche.
230. The Prophet Daniel.   Painting 29
     Northern drum of the cross
     vault.
231. The Three Holy Infants. Mo-
     saic. Southern drum of the cross
     vault. Painting on the front
     cover.

II. CHURCH OF THE VIRGIN

A. Temple. Iconostasis. Floor.

   1. Marble Temple with sculptural decoration.
   2. Marble plate on the floor.

B. Arched aperture between the Sanctuary and the
Diakonikón.

   3. Agios Ignatios Ceoforos. Fresco.
   4. Agios Polícarpos. Fresco.

C. Diakonikón, right from Sanctuary.

   5. Agios Jarálambos, fresco.
   Northern middle of the chamber.
   6. Agios Leon the Katanis, fresco.
   Northern middle of the chamber.
   7. Agios Sofronios, fresco.
   Northern middle of the chamber.

III. «CRYPT»

According to the way of construction the Crypt houses eleven spaces which on the plan are described with the capital letters *A-L* (the capital letter *I* is however omitted).

As to avoid repetitions, you will have to bear in mind that all decorative paintings in the Crypt are in full colour (frescoes) and also that «Agios» means «Saint» and «Apóstolos» means «Apostle».

A. Chamber just after the entrance.
1. Hosioi. Left middle of the arch.   Painting 30
2. Blessing Christ.
   In the middle of the arch.
3. Hosios Lukás.
   In the right middle of the arch.

B. Cross vault besides *A*.
4. Agios Aníkitos.   Painting 31
5. Agios Arezas.   Painting 31
6. Agios Fotios.   Painting 31
7. Agios Vikentios.   Painting 31

C. The southwesterly chamber with low vault, left, west from *E*.
8. Agios Máximos. Vault.
9. Agios Abramios. Vault.
10. Agios Doroceos. Vault.
11. Agios Ceoctistos. Vault.
12. Closed door (The Incredulity of   Painting 32
    Thomas). Southern wall.
13. Hosios Lukás, Abbot Basilios and
    Blessing Christ. Western wall.

D. Western cross vault from central side between *C* and *E*.
14. Apóstolos Ioanis the Theologian.
15. Apóstolos Petros.
16. Apóstolos Paulos.
17. Apóstolos Barzolomeos.

E. Northwesterly cross vault, North from *D*.
18. Agios Sisois.
19. Agios Ioaníkios.

20. Agios (unknown).
21. Agios Makarios.
22. The «Kímisis of the Virgin».
    Northern wall.

F. Cross vault, East from *E*, in front of the entrance.
   23. Agios (unknown).
   24. Agios (unknown).
   25. Agios (unknown).
   26. Agios Giorgios.
   27. The Tomb of Hosios Lukás.
       Northern wall.

G. Cross vault, South from the latter, between *F* and *B*.
   (Central part).
   28. Agios Nestor.
   29. Agios Merkurios.
   30. Agios (?) (soldier).
   31. Agios (?) (soldier).

H. Northeasterly angular department.

32. Agios Lukás. Cross vault.	Painting 33
33. Agios Filoceos. Cross vault.	Painting 33
34. Agios Azanasios. Cross vault.	Painting 33
35. Agios Zeodosios. Cross vault.	Painting 33
36. Palms. Northern wall.	Painting 33
37. The Crucifixion.	Painting 33
Eastern wall.	and 34
38. The Sarcophagus. Southern part.	

J. South from the latter cross vault between *H* and *A*.
   (Central part).

39. Apóstolos Lukás.	Painting 35
40. Apóstolos Markos.	Painting 35
41. Apóstolos Andreas.	Painting 35
42. Apóstolos Matceos.	Painting 35

K. Southeasterly angular department.
   43. «Hosios páter emón Azanasios».
       Cross vault.
   44. «Hosios páter emón Zeodosios».
       Cross vault.
   45. «Hosios páter emón Filoceos».
       Cross vault.

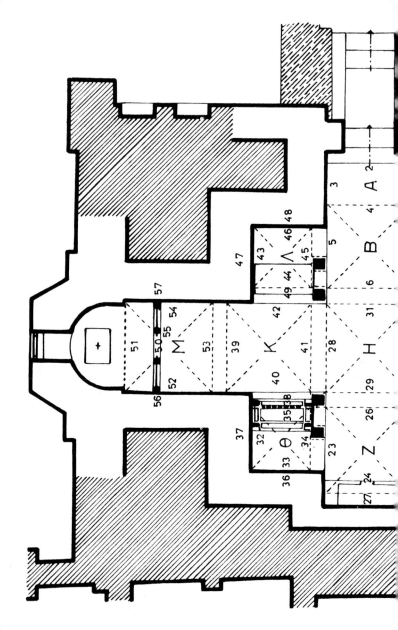

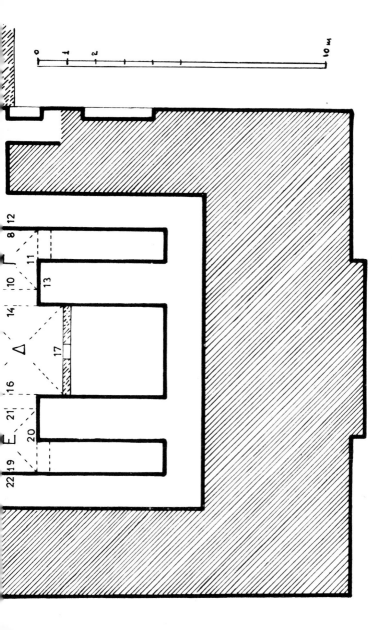

HOSIOS LUKAS. MONASTERY

Position.

The Monastery of Hosios Lukas, the magnificent center of spirituality and monastic life in Greece during the Byzantine and Postbyzantine periodes, is located on the western slope of Mount Helikonas, between Beocia and Fokida.

The founder

The Monastery was founded by Hosios Lukas «the Steiriotes». His parents originated from the Island of Egina. It was to escape from the Sarracens that they left the island and settled down in Fokida, near Mount Yanitsa —now called Yannimakia, on the coast of Kiras—. After some years, they went to Kastorion —the old Kastri, now Delphi—. There, in 896 a.C., was born Hosios Lukas. From his childhood he was inclined to ascetic life. When he was 14 years old, he left to Attica together with two monks.

He used to go to the most isolated and recondite places in order to lead a strict ascetic life. Till 945, year of his settlement in the place where he founded the Monastery, he lived for 35 years in the Church of the Anargiros Saints in Yannimakia (till 917), with ascetics in Zemenos and Patras (917-927), once again in Yannimakia (927-939), afterwards in Kalami, near the Gulf of Antikiras (939-942), and finally on an isolated island from the Gulf of Corinth, called Ambelaki, on cape Zaltsa (942-945).

From 945 till the day of his death (7th February 953) he lived in that marvellous place where he founded his Monastery, below the Acropolis of the old Steirion, on the place where stood the Sanctuary of Demetra. In 955 of our time, the day of his death was commemorated for the first time.

The buildings

The Monastery is constituted by the cells, which have two and three stories, and also by the four auxiliar places: the tower of the belfrey on the southwesterly corner, the reconstructed «Trapeza» on the south side, and the two temples with the Crypt, in the center of the building. It is to remark that, owing to the inclination of the ground, the shape of the Monastery is not quadrat but makes an irregular body of five sides —length of the north side: 83 meters, west side: 46.50 meters, east side 35.50 meters, and the total length of the two southern sectors: 70.50 meters—.

According to some links from the life of Hosios Lukas, to written testimonies, and also to the tradition, when he arrived in this place, where the Monastery stands nowadays, he found a fountain, that is still in front of the Nave entrance, near which he built his cell and arranged a garden to grow pot-herbs. After a short time, his name beings spread all over the country, a lot of other ascetics joined him. Then they were forced to build more cells and a small Church.

The help forwarded by pious christians, normally ill people cured in this place thanks to the supernatural atrength of Hosios Lukas, and also by generous and rich officials, generals, etc., afforded Hosios Lukas and his ascetics the possibility to build a great temple, which, following the wish of Hosios Lukas, was consecrated to Saint Barbara. This temple is on the North —the smallest one from the two composing the Monastery—, now devoted to the Virgin.

Hosios, apart from his curative and thaumaturge attitudes, possessed also the gift of the prophecy. He predicted, among other things, the invasion of the Bulgarians, the liberation of the Island of Crete from arabic occupation, his own death, etc.

The liberation of the Island of Crete in 961 of our time was the main factor for the divulgation and respect of his name and the reason why the Monastery was enriched by valuable gifts and real prerogatives.

31

After a few years (1011 a.C.) Abbot Filoceos and Ascetics Gabriel, Gregorius and Petros built the second great temple —the Nave— to the memory of Hosios Lukas. In this temple was placed a case with the reliquaries of Hosios Lukas.

From the old cells there are very few parts left, specially the covered places on the western and septentrional sides of the ground floor which, at different periods, were the foundations for the construction of two and three stories that changed the initial look of the Monastery. The old cells have only a door and a window on the façade. The main entrance, still preserved but not used any more, is on the northwest side of the premises where today one can see the following buildings: a) «Vordonareion», to the east, long building with a row of four arches alongside the longitudinal axis used as stable for the mules of the Monastery, and b) «Fotanama», to the west, with chambers and vaults that supported four monolithic columns. In the chimney of «Fotanama» the fire continiously burnt and the monks used to seat in front of it during the winter months to get warm.

At a distance of 7 meters from the south of the Nave is located the «Trapeza» of the Monastery (27.10 × 10.5 meters) which was destroyed in 1943 by a bombardment and newly reconstructed. The Nave and the former «Trapeza» were built at the same period. It consists of two stories. The superior one is the «Trapeza», place where the monks used to eat. From the 18th century the internal and external aspect of the «Trapeza» changed completely.

During the works of reconstruction the following frescoes, belonging to the 18th century, were discovered on its walls: In the smallniche, the Virgin and Child, Hosios Lukas, the Sacrifice of Abraham, an Archangel, an imperial figure, possibly Romanos the 2nd, who according to the monks of the 17th and 18th centuries, was the founder of the Monastery, and the Hospitability of Abraham.

The lower part of the building (heigth 5.10 meters and width 8.30 meters) is divided by a row of three twin columns into two places. It was employed as a store and also as a kind of workshop, because there big casks for liquors, a wine press and other items were found.

South from the «Trapeza» are located the ruins of the hospital which was built in the 17th century.

Between the Nave and the «Trapeza» is the subterranean «Kisterna» —water reservoir— which, owing to a colonnade alongside the axis and to six arches, is divided into eight quadrat apartments, each one of them being covered by a low arched vault. By its shape, one can assume that this water reservoir was one of the first buildings from the Monastery —11th century—.

Outside the western corner from the cells of the Monastery was, till about 1890, «the Circular Tower of Andrutsos». There is nothing left nowadays.

Another quadrat tower on the northeasterly corner of «Vordonareion» has also disappeared.

From the three towers initially composing the Monastery, there is only the quadrat tower of four stories, on the southwesterly corner over the entrance, that, being built later on, has been preserved. At the beginning, this tower had not the actual form, as it was only composed of two stories. The ground floor (5.35×5.35 meters), covered by a cross vault was employed as a water reservoir.

The second story was quadrat and its construction, owing to the four arches and the counter-forts on the four corners, had the shape of an octagon over which were the drum and the semicircular vault.

On the east side one could see the semihexagonal arch projected to the outside. It was destroyed in the 19th century, being its ruins found during the works that took place in 1960.

For all the reasons exposed, one can say that there was an octagonal temple similar to the Nave of the Monastery.

Inside there are still some paintings from its decoration. The scenes show the miracles worked by Christ, specially the cures.

The materials employed for its construction and also its shape and the painting show that this small temple of two stories was built at the same time as the one of Hosios

Lukas, i. e., at the beginning of the 11th century. Later on, between 1460 and 1569, another story was added and it became a defense tower.

Its actual shape dates to 1860 and in 1877 a clock was placed on it.

The entrance to the Monastery takes place today through a small and arched portico in the southern enclosure below the already mentioned tower. On a plan left behind in 1745 by the monk and traveller from Kiev, Basilios Plakas —Barskij—, there are shown this portico as well as a story with cells for the monks, in great number at the time.

THE TWO TEMPLES AND THE CRYPT

a) CHURCH OF THE VIRGIN

In the middle of the room located between the open air, i. e. room which was at the time encircled by the cells and the other buildings, raise the two majestic Temples of the Monastery: The Church of the Virgin on the left, and the Temple of Hosios Lukas on the right.

These two temples are linked in a way which is not very frequent. The southern wall from the hall and portico of the Church of the Virgin and the eastern half of the northern wall from the Temple of Hosios Lukàs are entangled in such a way that it is hard to make out which of the walls belong to each of the two temples. (See plan *a.*)
However, from the studies and discoveries made during the works carried out by the Archaeological Service for the preservation and construction of the buildings of the Monastery, it has been proofed without any kind of doubts that the small temple, the one of the Virgin, was built at a later date than the big one.

Its construction started in 946 of our time —Hosios Lukas was still alive—, thanks to the economical help of the Greek General Krinitos, who was a great admirer of Hosios Lukas. His pupils ended in 955, two years later from

34

the death of Hosios Lukas, the works of reconstruction. This temple was initially consecrated to Saint Barbara.

The Temple has four columns in the shape of a cross vault with an altar completely altered. On the eastern wall of the altar there are three semicircular niches in the inside and semihexagonal in the outside. To the west, there is a large space in front of the steps of the altar whose low and arched vaults are supported by two columns of granite. Later on, was added a portico covered by five cross vaults. The southern one was incorporated to the Temple of Hosios Lukas.

The Temple underwent often severe damages and renovations. In 1790 it nearly fell down owing to an earthquake and it was necessary to support it in 1848. In 1870-1871 all the inside was painted and filled with frames, decorations and other ornaments made with plaster cast, changing the look of the Temple. In 1971 all the decorations, ruined by the time elapsed, that did not belong to the epoch of the construction were removed, restablishing in this way its primitive form.

While doing this last restauration, it was very interesting to discover the way how the inside walls were built: they employed porose stones separated by bricks placed in horizontal series. Different paintings and sculptures were also made out.

From the frescoes, there are only left the one of Saint Ignatios, the Teoforos, and the Policarpos, on the arched portico between the Pulpit (figure 1, B, 3-4), and the Diakonikon, and the ones of Saint Jarálambos, Leon the Katanis, and the Sofronios on the north side of the Diakonikon (figure 1, C, 5, 6 and 7). From all these few samples of decoration from the church of the Virgin, we can say that these paintings, all of them preserved till the earthquake from 1790 and some till 1850, dated to the 11th or the 12th century.

A fresco with the representation of the Christ of Navi, lately discovered on the eastern wall of the vaulted corridor in the northern ground floor of the great temple, place of communication with the portico from the Church of The

Virgin, gives us possibly a sample of the first decoration in this temple (figure 1, *C*, number 175, Painting 24). The Christ of Navi belongs, in fact, to the Church of the Virgin, because the wall, on whose surface it is painted, supports the western part of this Church, which was at the time free and visible before the construction of the Temple of Hosios Lukas. Bearing in mind that, during the time of construction of this new Temple, part of the composition from the Christ of Navi was destroyed and that the part left was covered by a marble plate from the great Temple, one comes to the conclusion that the fresco was painted before 1011 of our time, year of construction of the Temple of Hosios Lukas.

For the reason above exposed, we must place it in the second half of the 10th century. The figure of the Christ of Navi shows real virility and severity, characteristics that the art has developped after the time of the «fights for the icons» and therefore constitutes the echo of the atmosphere that prevailed in the second half of the 10th century, during the Byzantine Empire, time of the continous fights between the Goverment and the Pagans. The Christ of Navi, painted on the outside wall of the Temple of Saint Barbara, as at the time the Church of the Virgin was called, was a kind of shield against the beligerous Arabs and Bulgarians.

From the sculptural decoration of the Church of the Virgin, there are only left: the four pilasters, the arch of the frame of Christ's figure in the southern part of the Sancturay, the marble temple, and the highly interesting story covered with marble.

The four pilasters do not belong to the same style. There are some in the shape of the well-known corinthian style with the erected leaves and other kinds of decorative compositions. The others have bright and fine leaves that cover their surface and figures of Cherubs on the top, etc. The decorations in the Temple and on the picture-frame of Jesus were finished with great care.

The high technical quality and the aesthetic finess of the sculptures of the Virgin are related with the Greek

36

micographic manuscripts that date to about 950 of our time.

The outside of the Church of the Virgin could be described as being one of the best architectural and decorative samples from the Byzantine art (Painting 40, right). The careful way of stone construction with the colourful porose stones, the arched apertures of one, two and three arches at different levels, the roofs, the elegant though modified vault, the rich ceramic decoration with the continous superposition of ribbons and the various compositions systematically disposed, interlacing the flat and luminous stones, are the reason why the Church of the Virgin is distinguished as the most perfect and accomplished monument from the middle of the 10th century of our time (about 950). Thanks to this Church we look at the artistic problems of that century in a different way.

b) THE TEMPLE OF HOSIOS LUKAS (Nave)

For a reason of religiousness and respect to the memory of the Monastery's founder, and also for a practical reason, the need of free space for the numerous pilgrims that usually were sleeping there, another temple of bigger proportions was built under the appelation of Hosios Lukas.

The construction of this new Church started at the beginning of the 11th century of our time, and was finished about 1011. There was on the 3rd of May, under the Abbot Filoceos and his ascetics Gabriel, Gregorios and Petros, when the rests of Hosios Lukas were collected from his grave, laid under the new temple, in the marble shrine which they put into a case exactly in the place where the old Church of the Virgin and the new one join (figure *a*, position *S*, number 176). The magnificency of the Church of Hosios Lukas and its rich ornamentation produced, and still produce, surprise and wonder and justify the thought that this work could not have been done without an important aid from the Emperor. For this, the tradition establishes a relationship, though without any reason, between the graves

37

of the Crypt and the Emperor Romanos the 2nd and his wife.

The new Church has an octagonal shape, being its main feature the big dome of 9.00 meters of diameter and 5.25 meters of height. This dome is based, by the means of a drum of 16 sides, each one having a window, on four strong pillars that are formed on the corners of the walls of the big square —see the plan— and on the four arches of the roof (figure *a*, position *J*).

There are no inside supports —columns— for the dome. The weight and continuity follow a marvellous order with arches on the outside walls and in the chapels on the four corners of the building (figure *a*, positions *F* and *H* and the ones in the East).

With all this, a large free space appears inside the Church. This enormous building, nevertheless, does not look heavy or melancholic, because its walls are open by two or three arches and, furthermore, outside, they are lightened by the means of large windows with two or three arches and a lot of glass windows in the Byzantine style.

The small arches are supported by light marble columns and the apertures are closed by nice sculptural ornamentations. The exterior view of the building, in spite of its huge volume, produces also an agreable feeling (Painting 40 and back cover).

For the construction of the lower parts of the walls, the builders used marble, epigraphs and other materials from the buildings of the old Steirion, while on the upper parts we can see the dentated series carried out with bricks and porose stones carefully squared that are embraced by reddish stones. The shape of the Temple, the harmonious combination of its volumes, and the artistic ornamentation even shown on its smaller parts, give this Church a lightness and a charm that make of it the most perfect sample of the octagonal style, that was afterwards adopted by other temples, i. e. Sotira Likodimu of Athens, second half of the 11th century, Daphni, end of the 11th century, etc.

What makes, nevertheless, the Church of Hosios Lukas to go ahead from the other Byzantine monuments of Greece, is its marvellous ornamentation of paintings: the mosaics and frescoes. The upper parts of the walls, the chambers, the cross vaults, the shields, the drums of the windows and many other spots of the Temple and the Narthex are decorated with mosaics, while the chapels and the drum with frescoes. The other surfaces of the walls are covered with marble plates of big proportions and a large variety of colours.

The classification of the scenes, of the isolated figures and the different themes, follow the order in which the decoration of paintings in the churches was done, after the end of the so called «Iconomachy». This ornamentation has a close relationship with the symbolical and allegorical scenes of the Church, according to which, it symbolizes the Univers and is, therefore, the House of God. «Eklesia estín epigéios uranós, en o Epuranios ceós enoikei kai emperipatei» (Germanós from Constantinopolis, 730 of our time). On the dome, the Almighty God, the King of Heaven and Earth, is surrounded by the celestial army and His officers, while downstairs, in the temple, the World is represented as a big crowd of Saints and Martyrs, all who worked and fought for the glory of the King of Heaven.

The evangelical scenes are very limited, as they were not necessary: Four in the Narthex —the Crucifixion, the Baptism, the Resurrection, and the Incredulity of Saint Thomas—, and only five in the Temple —The Evangelicism, The Nativity, «Ipapantí», Baptism and Whitsuntide—.

We can now see the most important iconographical themes:

a)   *Narthex* (see classification I, a figure *a*, plans *A*, *B*, *C*, numbers 1-42, Paintings 1-9).

The visitor who enters the narthex contemplates immediatly on the arched drum, beneath the door towards the temple, the severe but quiet figure of Christ in the golden field showing, as the Master of the Church, by the open Gospel, that He is the only light of the world. The neck of Christ looks very strong through the yellow tunic. Jesus

Christ is sidefaced. If one imagines this whole body, the feet would touch the upper part of the door, so that the one who comes into the temple would walk under His feet (figure *a*, position *A*, number 1, Paintings 1 and 2).

Inside a medallion on each one of the four triangles of the cross vault and above Christ, are represented the Virgin, John Prodromos and the two Archangels (Painting 2). They are the direct surrounding of the Great Master. With their gentle expression, they are giving courage to the christian people. On the same cross vault and in front of Christ, there are five Saints holding the cross of the Martyrdom: Anembódistos, Pigasios, Akíndinos, Afzonios and Elpidoforos (figure *a*, position *A*, numbers 6-10).

On the northern cross vault, on the four triangular sides, are represented in medallions the Saints Physicians Kosmas, Damianós, Kiros and Ioannis, and on the vertical surfaces: to the East, the Crucifixion, to the North the Feet Lavatory and to the West six holy women, three of them in full-length: Irini, Ekaterina, and Barbara, and the other three in medaillons Euphemia, Marina and Juliana (figure *a*, position *B*, numbers 14-18, 22 and 23-28; Paintings 3, 4, 5).

The representation of the Crucifixion —painting 3— is very simple but at the same time dramatic and noble. From the end of the 9th century and the beginning of the 10th century, the style has been modified, specially in the micographical works, according to which dead Jesus appears with the eyes closed and the figure submerged in a mournful peacefulness. The works that follow this style only represent the three main figures of the drama: Jesus, the Virgin and John. Here, in the Church of Hosios Lukas, we can discover the oldest sample of this great painting: the mosaics of the walls (beginning of the 11th century).

In the golden field towards the center of the drum, stands out the Crucified with a light inclination of the body to the left. He wears a piece of cloth around His hips, and His feet are firmly based on the cross. Through the right side of His body flow water and blood, the arms are extended with ease along the cross, while the head with the eyes closed, once Christ pronounced that terrible «tetelestai», is slightly inclined over the right shoulder. By the sides of the cross, at a lower and smaller level than the figure of Christ, the Virgin shows the distress she feels at the sight of Her beloved Son, hanging from the cross, raising the right hand with a painful look, and John demonstrates his affliction by putting his right hand on his head. We must say that it is not possible to present a better expression of God's greatness in this dramatic moment.

The scene of the Lavatory of the Feet is shown following the style already created on the 6th century of our time (Painting 4).

In the center of the scene we can see the two most important figures, Jesus and Petros, and behind them, in two groups, the Apostles. Jesus slightly inclined, does not wear the towel —«lention»— on the waist, but on the hands to dry Petros feet. The latter, with his right hand on the head, means that, so as to be always with Jesus, he is disposed to allow Him to wash even his head. The other pupils are also getting ready, while at the same time they show their surprise, by the movements of their heads, for all that is happening. In the southern appartement of the narthex, the four medaillons of the cross vaults are destroyed. On the vertical surfaces are represented: to the East, the Resurrection, to the South, the Incredulity of Thomas, and to the West, the raising of the Cross by Saint Costantinos and Saint Helena and five Holy Martyrs, each one inside a medaillon: Thekla, Agatha, Anastasia, Febronia and Eugenia (figure a, position C, numbers 32, 36, 37-42, paintings 7, 8 and 9).

The Resurrection (Painting 37), that is to say, «The Descension to Hell», as the bizantine tradition says, is a symetric and equilibrated representation. As it is well known, Jesus, during the three days that He was buried, came down to hell to destroy its power and to raise those who were sleeping from centuries.

The main figure of the composition is constituted by the body of Jesus who wears a golden tunic and a white cape flying in the wind.

With the right hand He holds a high cross and with the left pulls out from their grave —a sarcophagus in decorated marble— our first parents, Adam and Eve. To the left, the two crowned prophets, David and Solomon, who had prophesied this happening.

The representation of the Incredulity Of Thomas is also symmetrical. Jesus stands in front of the closed door —ton círon kekleismeno— raises with a majestic gesture His right hand and shows His right side. Thomas, who has his head broken, puts the forefinger of his right hand into the sore, while the other ten Apostles —Judas the traitor does not appear on the scene—, distributed in two groups at the sides of the door, watch the scene with some dread (Painting 8).

The twelve Apostles are represented on the arches dividing the three cross vaults of the Narthex. Eight of them are standing up on the arch bases: Petros, Paulos, Andreas, Matheos, Lukas, Ioannis the Theologian, Thomas, and Philip, while the other four Marcos, Simon, Iacobos and Bartolomeos are inside the medaillons placed in the center of the four arches. (Figure *a*, position *A*, *B*, *C*, numbers 11-13, 19-21, 29-31, 33-35. Paintings 4, 6, 8.)

These are the disciples of the Divine Teacher, who preached His Doctrine and founded the Christian Churches that are spread all over the world.

b-c) *The main Temple and the Sanctuary.*

As we have already said, the pictorial decoration of the Temple consists of mosaics and frescoes.

I) Mosaics

Only four scenes of the cycle «Dodecaortos» are preserved —The Evangelicism, on the northeastern squinch is destroyed—. On the southeastern squinch, we can see the Nativity. This scene, whose first representations come from the paleo-christian period, has been worked out in a new style. There are all the known elements: The Virgin slightly inclined over the Child in the cradle, the two animals to the right, the scene of the bath with the two women, four shepherds with their sheep, to the upper part two Angels and to the left Joseph seating and looking at the cradle; The Magi who are walking towards Christ and three other angels at the highest level. This composition shows symmetry, movement and logical distribution of the figures, as well as a high harmony of colour. More simple is the scene of «Ipapanti» (Painting 20). Simeon facing the conic «Kivorion» supported by green columns, extends his covered hands to receive the Saviour of the World, brought by the Virgin, while a little further Joseph holds a couple of pigeons. Behind Simeon, the Prophetess Ann blesses with her right hand and watches the scene with thrill. The golden shining field gives the feeling that the five figures of the scene are moving in front of a fire.

The scene of the Baptism is also another sample of symmetry and unity (Painting 21). In the center of the painting, formed by the body of Jesus, the hand that blesses from Heaven and a bright shaft of light, Jesus is represented without dresses. The characteristic representation of the water covers partially his «Nudity» Ioannis, on the right bank of the Jordan extends his hands over the head of Jesus, and on the left bank two angels, holding a folded cloth, wait to dry the body of Jesus. There is also a little figure of an old man in the water that personifies the River Jordan. The scene is completed by the tree with the axe in its bottom.

The Whitsuntide fills the lower vault, above the Holy Pulpit. Unfortunately, half of the scene is destroyed. In the center of the golden vault, in a disc of a deep blue colour, is represented the Revealing Theme of the «Throne Preparation». This vacant throne fully decorated with the Gospel in it, symbolizes the Second Presence of the Lord. The arrival of the Holy Spirit during the Whitsuntide is represented over the throne under the form of a pigeon. The Apostles, seating in the thrones, disposed in a circular manner, receive the Holy Spirit in form of fire fingers.

The Apostles present a certain movement and life with their heads looking at different directions and the rich folds of their dresses, many of which are rised up by the wind. We can still see that the figures of the Apostles are real portraits, with the personal features on each of them.

Around, though seriously damaged, there are groups of people congregated in Jerusalem for the Feasts of Whitsuntide, and the words «Filai» (races) and «Glossai» (languages) can still be read.

In the fourth circle of the shield of the Sanctuary, in the golden sky, the «Platitera» is represented in a throne scarcely touching little Jesus with a hand full of tenderness. This shield is the part that joins the Temple to the floor, that is, Heaven to the Earth. For this reason, this place was consecrated to the Virgin that joined the celestial to the terrestrial. The figure of the Virgin shines with outstanding beauty and majesty (figure *a*, plan, position *U*, number 183).

In the small cavities formed in the vertical walls of the inside square of the Temple under the four squinches, are represented two Chiefs of the Christian Spirit and the Greek education, Basilios and Ioannis Jrisostomos, two of the founders of the Orthodox Faith, Nikolaos and Gregorios the «Thaumaturgus».

These four stoical figures are full of spirit (figure *a*, plan, positions *K*, *L*, *M* and *N*, numbers 120, 127, 131 and 135, Paintings 17 and 19).

In the Diakonikon —the covered space in the southern part of the main Temple— two important representations can be seen: «The Prophet Daniel in the Lions' Den» and «The Three Infants». These are two of the themes that the paleo-christian art has taken from the Old Testament and that those artists liked to paint on the frescoes of the Catacombs, and the micrographic works, etc. Their contents had a close relationship with the faith and mentality of the former christians: suffering the torments without plaints, victory of the faith over the violence and the persecutions, etc. These scenes were beloved above all because they symbolized the Passion, Death and Resurrection of Jesus (figure *a*, plan, position *X*, 216-231, Paintings 28 and 29, and on the front cover).

Dozens of Saints, Martyrs, Chiefs of the Church, etc. are represented, in the medallions or in full length, on all the surfaces of the upper building, of the chambers and the cross vaults, between earth and heaven (about 150, before the destruction of the mosaics).

It is to remark a special preference for the monastic and military scenes. We may assume that the decoration of the Temple has been done in a period of strong fights between the Empire and several enemies. The figures represented are formed by the armies that fought and were sacrified for the Orthodox Faith and the Glory of God.

As an instance, we can refer to some characteristic figures: Agios Panteleimon, in the western drum of the cross vault of the southern door (figure *a*, plan, position *Q*, number 156); Agios Nikos, the «Metanoite», who visited the Monastery in 982, in the cross vault by the south of the door —western wall— (figure *a*, plan, position *E*, number 48, painting 10); Agios Lukas, the «Gurnikiotis», in the cross vault by the north of the same entrance —western wall— (figure *a*, plan, position *G*, number 77, Painting 14); and Agios lukas, «The Steiriotes», the founder of the Monastery, in the cross vault near the northern entrance —western wall—, precisely in front of the «Kivorion» and the case containing the bones of the Saint (figure *a*, plan, position *S*, number 171, Painting 23). If to this great amount of representations referred to up to now, we add the rich decoration with large profussion of subjects, as flowers, plants, geometrical and free disigns, etc. that is spread all over the Church, so as there is no space without decoration, one may be convinced why the Temple of Hosios Lukas has been distinguished as the most important monument among those decorated with mosaics.

II) Frescoes

The mosaics are one of the parts of the so called «great painting», and the frescoes the other one. The mosaic is a very expensive work, being destined, owing to the nature of the materials that were used for their confection (glasses of various colours, silver, gold, etc.), to the higher places, distant from the spectator. They all must be placed in a different inclination and be exposed to sufficient natural light, because only in this way their colours can be interpreted in their complete brightness. Thus, the mosaic, by the reflexion of the light, gives the impression of a sky full of thousands of stars.

For this reason, the decoration in the back grounds of the Temple of Hosios Lukas, as the «ginaikonites», or in the rather dark places, for instance, the angles of the chapels (position *F* and *H*, and the ones to the east, figure *a*, plan), has been completed with frescoes.

The decoration of the drum is not included in all that has been already said, because it is, as we explain later, more recent.

These frescoes were recently cleaned up and restaured by the Archaeological Service and, therefore, those beautiful works, contemporary of the mosaics, appear nowadays in full splendour.

At the beginning the enormous drum of the Temple (8.96 meters of diameter and over 5.22 meters of height) was decorated with mosaics in the same way as all the other surfaces of the upper building, with the same themes and order: The Pantocrator, The Angels and the Prophets. These mosaics fell down after the earthquakes of 1593. The period of the tyrannic oppression by the Sovereign and the robbery of the Governors and their Officials was not suitable for the construction of too expensive works. For this reason, the drum was decorated with frescoes. Not so long ago, several techniciens stressed that the frescoes of the drum had been painted around 1820, when really, according to the epigraphs, only some restauration works were carried out. During the works done in 1971 by the experts of the Archaeological Services for the reinforcement and cleaning of the frescoes, it was confirmed without any doubt, once the superposed coats of paint were taken away, that the pictorial decoration of the drum was completed by the end of the 16th century, probably a few years after the destruction of the mosaics in 1553. The incontestable proofs for this assertion are the golden colour of the field that has appeared under the later colours, the inscriptions and the careful work done.

The Pantocrator is of a supernatural size. Here are some of his measurements: Length of the eyes, 0,24 meters; height of the nose, 0.43 meters; length of the forehead, 1.35 meters; height of the Gospel, 1.10 meters; length of the Gospel, 0.79 meters; inside diameter of the aureole —drawing a direct line—, 2.05 meters, and inside diameter of the circle —in straight line where the figure is represented, 3.92 meters. Jesus Pantocrator does not present the grim expression of the terrible judge of the human acts, although this expression was common in the figure of the Pantocrator in the middle of the Byzantine period (11th and 12th century, Monastery of Daphni). Afterwards, owing to the oppression that the Greek people suffered by the Turks, the face of Christ became more benign and placid. Below, 2.50 m. of height, are represented: The Virgin, Ioannis Prodromos, as the angel incarnate, and four Archangels —«Generals of the celestial army»—. The height of these figures is 2.25 m. This is the direct surrounding of King Jesus. On the third zone of the drum, that constitutes its support —2.54 m. high— and between the 16 arches of the windows (2.12 × 0.85 meters), seven of which are blind, are represented the 16 Prophets, who prophesied the Nativity, the Life and the Passion of the Messiah and prepared the humanity for His coming.

Very interesting and heavy is the pictorial decoration of the chapel in the south west angle of the ground floor. Ten Saints in the medallions, seven in full-length, the blessing hand of God, the Virging in full-length with Jesus, under the form of the «leading woman», Jesus with Ioannis Prodromos, as well as beautiful vegetal and geometrical subjects cover all the surfaces of the walls, the chamber, the cross vault and the niche (figure a, plan, position F, numbers 57-176, Paintings 11-13).

Graceful is also the imitation of the Church, that remainds

of the popular art, in the drum of the two arched window in the southern wall. The Virgin, holding Jesus to the left side, looks at Him with a stoical expression and guesses the terrible torments that He was to suffer (Painting 12).

The representation of Jesus with Ioannis Prodromos is very characteristic. This is the scene before the Baptism takes place. Ioannis, showing his surprise by the means of a movement of his hand, says «I must be baptised by Thee and Thou are coming to me!» And Jesus, who wears a green tunic, blesses Ioannis and walks in a blue field, saying: «afes arti uto gar prepon sten plerosai pasan dikaiosinen» —the original ortograph is respected— (Painting 13). A greater unity and more accurate plan, as corresponds to the decorative painting of a small temple, present the frescoes of the chapel in the north east angle of the building (figure *a*, plan, position *H*, numbers 90-117, Painting 15).

There is a very important and characteristic group of frescoes —the work of an artist— constituted by the Pantocrator, in the low vault, the Transfiguration, on the eastern wall, the Crucifixion, on the southern wall, the «Analipsis of Ilios», on the western wall, below Jesus, as Emmanuel, the two Archangels Mijail and Gabriel, in the dividing arch, and 20 Saints, below the Transfiguration, in full-length and in the medallions, among them Hosios Lukas, the founder of the Monastery.

In the north east chapel (figure *a*, plan, north from *V*), that is, the longitudinal space formed at the joining point of the two temples, the one of the Virgin and the one of Hosios Lukas, that was used, it has been confirmed, as a passage for the ill pilgrims, very few frescoes have been preserved: The Virgin holding the Child, Agios Kiriakos, Agios Nikolaos and two other Agios, Hosios Lukas on the western wall above the case that contains his reliquaries, and, once again, Hosios Lukas with a monk who offers him the Imitation of The Church. This last representation has a great importance, because it shows the characteristics of the man who offered the gift, tha Abbot Filoteos. The latter has been also represented, as we have said before, in the Crypt. The frescoes, shown in a brief way, are the work of at least two painters. They are most important for the quality of the achievement and also as they constitute the last «touch» of the decorative painting of the great temple, almost from the same epoch as the mosaics or from a few years later.

The few frescoes of the «Protesis», north from the main sanctuary —figure a, plan, position V, numbers 194-212—, are not of great interest, because, if we trust the inscriptions on the southern wall, they have been carried out in 1820, on the iniciative and protection of the «Saint Abbot Lord Eugenios» (sculptures, portable icons).

The marvellous decoration —mosaics and frescoes— from the inside of the great temple of Hosios Lukas is completed by the beautiful designs and the marble plates of the floor (OPUS ALEXANDRINUM) as well as in the northern and southern entrances and in the sanctuary (figure a, plan, positions Q, S and U, numbers 159, 177 and 193, Painting 27), by the decorations of the upper construction with their fine sculptural work, the divisions between the marble building and the mosaics and the drum —paintings 16, 18, 20, 21 and 26—, the small capitals in the openings of two or three inside arches and the marble temple with its delicate and beautiful sculptural decoration, discovered some years ago under another which, being rougher, comes from a later period (figure a, plan, position T, number 178, Painting 25).

Finally, four portable icons must be mentioned: 1) Jesus Pantocrator, 2) The Virging holding the Child, «Everybody's Faith», in the style of the Virgin of the Passion, 3) Agios Ioannis Prodromos, and 4) Agios Lukas from «Sterios of Greece». These are the marvellous works done by the well-known cretan painter of the 16th century, Mijail Damaskinos (figure a, plan, position T, numbers 179-182, Painting 24).

They belong to the third group of Damaskinos' Icons, by which the real technique of the Cretan portable icon can be felt. The icons of this group have been carried out after 1571, epoch when the technique of Mijail Damaskinos is in its higher maturity (1571-1579).

The Crypt

Classification of the subjects & *III* (figure *b*, plan, *A-L*,
    numbers 1-57, paintings 30-39).

Owing to the natural declivity of the ground to the south,
the new temple of Hosios Lukas has been built at a lower
level than the first temple of the Virgin. This, nevertheless,
would damage the shape of the new building and, on the
other hand, the inequality of the grounds of both temples
would difficult the movements of the pilgrims. There were
only two possible ways out: to raise up the lower part of
the new temple, so as to have its floor at the same level as
the one of the Virgin's, or to create an underground building. The second solution was chosen. By the means of a
wide and strong constructions of walls and four supports
—the two eastern are twins— a subterranean space was
made in the shape of a cross with four angular departments.
As this space also comprehended the place where Hosios
Lukas had been buried, it was used afterwards as the grave
for the high personalities that inhabited the Monastery's
zone. It could be characterized as a graves' chapel, following the habitudes of the former Martyrs.
    Once the first temple became the one of the Virgin, the
Crypt was consecrated to Saint Barbara. Owing to its building style, the Crypt is divided into 14 departments, inclu-
ding also its chamber of the southern entrance. All these
departments are covered by a cross vault, but for the one
besides the entrance and the three at the west, that are covered by vaults, being the angular on the south west covered
by a low vault (figure *b*, plan).
    The frescoes of the Crypt can now be studied thanks to
the cleaning carried out by the specialists of the Archaeological Service. These frescoes are spread in the entrance
vault, in the cross vaults and on the surfaces of the walls
belonging to 11 departments; the other three departments
are covered by vaults (figure *b*, plan).
    The iconographic subjects that have escaped unscathed
up to this date are: 11 scenes on the walls, 40 medallions, 12

Apostles and 28 Saints on the cross vaults, a group of monks, two medallions of Jesus Christ, Hosios Lukas twice alone and once with a monk, and a diverse and wonderful decoration on the cross vaults and on the arches.

On the triangular surfaces of the three cross vaults (figure *b*, plan, positions *B*, *G* and *F*, numbers 4-7, 28-31 and 23-26, Painting 21), that are alongside the central axis, towards the north entrance, are represented in medallions, 12 Saints. On the three cross vaults that are longside the Cross axis (figure *b*, plan, positions *D*, *J* and *L*, numbers 14-17, 39-42, and 51-54, Paintings 35 and 38), are represented the medallions of the 12 Apostles. In the two south angular departments we can find 8 Saints (figure *b*, plan, positions *C* and *E*, numbers 8-11 and 18-21) and in the two eastern departments 4 figures of Saints, each one of them with the same names: Lukas, Filoceos, Azanasios and Zeodosios, with the only difference that, while in the northeast ones to the names the qualification «Agios» is added, in the south-east ones «Hosios pater emon» appears (figure *b*, plan, positions *H* and *K*, numbers 32-35 and 43-46, Paintings 33 and 36). It is evident that Hosios Lukas in the south-east department is among the most importante ascetics and the better-known abbots of the Monastery —we must remember that Filoceos is the founder of the great temple—. In the other group, north-east department, he is among the ancient Saints that have been identified. On the entrance arch are represented: on the right, Hosios Lukas blessing with his right hand; in the middle of the arch, Jesus in a medallion, blessing with both hands that come out from the circular frame; on the left, a group of 18-20 monks. In the first series, there are three tall monks, of respectable appearance; the first of them, on the left, is bareheaded, while the other two wear a hood, that proofs that they belong to the Great Order. This composition may have a double sense: the monks pray to Jesus through Hosios Lukas or perhaps the latter gives to the monks, with the blessing of Jesus, the Statutes according to which the Comunity of the Monastery must live. The three monks on the first rank can be identified as the three saints of the south-east angular deparment, Filoceos (the first from the left), Azanas and Zeodosios (figure *b*, plan, position *A*, numbers 1-3, Painting 30).

Once again Hosios Lukas is represented with a monk, probably the Abbot Basilios, and Jesus blessing (medallion), on the western wall of the angular department (figure *b*, plan, position *C*, number 13).

Nine of the scenes have been preserved up to our days, although partially some of them: 1) The Incredulity of Thomas, on the southern wall of the south-west angular department (figure *b*, plan, position *C*, number 12, Painting 32). 2) The Assumption of the Virgin, on the northern wall of the north-west angular department (figure *b*, plan, position *E*, number 22). 3) The «Vaioforos», on the northern wall of the north-east angular department (figure *b*, plan, position *H*, number 36, Painting 33). 4) The Crucifixion, on the eastern wall of the same department (number 37, Paintings 33 and 34). 5) The Descension of the Cross, on the eastern wall of the south-east angular department (figure *b*, plan, position *K*, number 47, Paintings 36 and 37). 6) The Burial of Jesus, on the southern wall of the same department (number 43, Painting 36). 7) The «Idete ton Tafon» —«Behold in the Tomb»—, on the same wall. 8) The Lavatory of the Feet, on the northern wall of the Sanctuary (figure *b*, plan, position *Z*, number 56). 9) The Lord's Supper, on the southern wall of the Sanctuary (figure *b*, plan, position *L*, number 57, Painting 39). The representation of the prayer in the niche of the Sanctuary does not exist any more.

The Incredulity of Thomas.—It presents the same order as the scene of the mosaic of the Narthex, with the difference that Jesus does not raise His right hand, but takes the hand of the doubting Thomas and approaches it to the wound of His side. This is a realistic element of the Oriental Art. One may observe that in this fresco there is more movement and a higher spirituality than in the mosaic of the Narthex (Painting 8 and 32).

The Assumption of the Virgin has undergone a lot of damages.

The «Vaioforos» is represented in the style of the 10th and 11th century: only the main figures appear: Jesus on the donkey, just followed by one of His disciples; two children and four Jewish men receive the Messiah at the doors of Jerusalem. In spite of the similitude that this scene has with one of the mosaics of the Monastery of Daphni, it has, however, a lower artistical and technical quality, as it belongs to the monastic art of the provinces.

The Crucifixion repeats the description made on the same scene of the mosaics of the Narthex, with the difference that the background is not monochrome —golden— like there, but it has been decorated with plants and mountains, and the head of Jesus has not fallen over His right shoulder, but is slightly depressed (Paintings 3 and 34).

The Descension of the Cross is one of the most beautiful and interesting representations of the Crypt. In front of the dark Cross, that glimmers in the blue field, the dramatic scene takes place. Nicodemos, after extracting the nails from the hands of the Crucified, is stooped and tries to remove the nails from the feet. Ioannis, behind, has the same position that he had in the Crucifixion; Joseph from Arimatea, climbed on the ladder in a less common position, holds out the Body of Jesus, as if It were not heavy, and, finally, the Virgin on the left corner, in the same position she had in the Crucifixion, does not express the dramatic movements as she did on other similar scenes, but she gently touches the right hand of Jesus. This scene represents the artistic style that has been developped during the 11th century and it may be considered as the best sample of the religious technical art (Painting 37).

The Burial of Jesus and the «Miroforas» in the grave are two wholy different episodes represented on this scene. To the left, Joseph and Nicodemos place with respect the Body of Jesus into the grave, while, behind, the Virgin with deep affliction bends towards Jesus without touching Him. This representation offers us a unique exemple of burial from the Byzantine epoch, in a very archaic style, with only two of the disciples, as in the ancient monuments of Capadocia (Painting 36).

53

On the other scene, the seating angel, with open wings, shows the empty grave to the «Miroforas». The representation follows the archaic style, as it has been developped in the 10th century.

The Lavatory of the Feet conserves the same order shown in the mosaic of the Narthex. The artist follows the hellenistic tradition (Painting 36).

Finally, the Lord's Supper belongs also to the archaic type of the scene, as it has been formed in the paleo-christian epoch: the Apostles are seating behind the arch, at a semicircular table, so that all of them are visible and Jesus is on the corner of the arch. Judas, in the center of the table, extends his hands to the fountain.

It has already been said that the frescoes of the Crypt have been recently cleaned up. They are, therefore, a theme of study and discussions. It is not the task of this book to study the theories and the views from the techniciens.

For this reason, we only expose the most important results:

a) The paintings have been done in two different periods. Some medallions of the abbots on the cross vaults and Hosios Lukas with the Abbot Basilios in the southwest angular department belong to the second period.

b) Two different artists and styles can be distinguished. One of the styles comprehends a lineal and figurative painting, like some of the mosaics. It could be characterized as oriental or monastic. The other style is more delicate, more fine and light. It follows and reproduces at the same time the hellenistic prototypes.

c) There are a lot of common elements mainly in the decoration as well as in the inspiration among the frescoes of the «ginaikonites», of the chapel of the great temple, specially the northern ones and those belonging to the Crypt.

d) The frescoes of the Crypt are very good elements to show us the level of the painting during the 11th century.

e) They do not constitute bare copies of the mosaics of the great temple, but they are their complement.

f) They are very original and valuable works done almost at the same time as the first decoration of the temple and they have been inspired on former Byzantine and Oriental works.

g) With a holy dignity, they express spiritual values.

h) They can be placed in the same epoch as the mosaics (about 1011 after Christ) or a little later on; anyway, in the first quarter of the 11th century.

The Temple of Hosios Loukas. View from the w

Ο Ναός του 'Οσίου Λουκά. Δυτική όψη.

Der Tempel von Hosios Lukas. Ansicht von Westen.

The Church of Hosios Loukas and the altar.

Ο Νεος του 'Οσιου Λουκά και η τράπεζα.

Die Kirche von Hosios Lukas und der Altar.

The Church of Hosios Loukas.
Ο Ναός του 'Οσιου Λουκά.
Die Kirche von Hosios Lukas.

The Tomb of Hosios Loukas.Crypt.
Ο Τάφος του Όσιου Λουκά. Κρύπτη.
Das Grab von Hosios Lukas. Krypta.

Saint Lucas Monastery : Virgin with Christ child on
her right. Mosaic. 11th c. A.D.

Μονή 'Οσίου Λουκά : Η Παναγία Δεξιοκρατούσα. Ψηφιδωτό.
11ος αι. μ.Χ.

Kloster des Heiligen Lukas : Die Jungfrau mit Christus
kind auf dem rechten. Mosaik. 11. Jh. n. Chr.

Saint Lucas Monastery : Jesus Christ. Mosaic.
11th c. A.D.

Μονή 'Οσίου Λουκᾶ : Ο Ιησούς Χριστός. Ψηφιδωτό.
11ος αι μ.Χ.

Kloster des Heiligen Lukas : Jesus Christus. Mosaik.
11. Jh. n. Chr.

Me(ter) C(eo)u. Virgin. Cross vault.
IE Arj(ággelos) Gabriel.
A(gios) Io(annis) o (Pró)dr(omos).
Cross vault.
Arj(ággelos) Mij(ail). Cross vault.

Πίνακας   2. Ἡ ἴδια παράσταση τοῦ Χριστοῦ καί στό σταυροθόλιο μέσα σέ κύκλους ἡ Παναγία, ὁ Ἀρχάγγελος Γαβριήλ ὁ Ἰωάννης ὁ Πρόδρομος καί ὁ Ἀρχάγγελος Μιχαήλ. Ψηφιδωτό. Νάρθηκας.

Mutter Gottes o. Panajïa. Kreuzgewlb.
Erzengel Gabriel. Kreuzgewlb.
Der hlg. Johannes der Vorläufer. Kreuzgewlb.
Erzengel Michael. Kreuzgewlb.

The Crucifixion. Drum of the Eastern arch.

Ost. —Bogenfeld— Die Kreuzigung.

A(gios) Matheos.
Eastern part of the septentrional arch.
Agios Simón. In the middle of the same arch.
A(gios) Lucás. Western part of the same arch.
Baptismal Font. Niche of northern wall.

Πίνακας 4. Ὁ Νιπτήρας (Ὁ Χριστός πλαίνει τά πόδια τῶν Μαθητῶν του).
Κόγχη βόρειου τοίχου. Ὁ Ἅγιος Λουκᾶς (ὁλόσωμος ἀριστερά),
ὁ Ἅγιος Σήμων (σέ κύκλο στό μέσο) καί ὁ Ἅγιος Ματθαῖος (ὁ-
λόσωμος δεξιά). Ἐσωράχιο βόρειου τόξου. Ψηφιδωτό. Νάρθηκας.

Der hlg. Matthäus- Ostschenkel des Bogens.
Der hlg. Simon. Im Zentrum des slb. Bogens.
Der hlg. Lukas- Westschenkel slb. Bogens.
Fusswaschung- Nische Nordwand.

ΟΜΑΤΘΑΙΟϹ

ΟΝΙΠΤΗΡ

ΟΛΟΥΚΑϹ

Agia Irene. Drum of western arch.
Agia Ekaterina. Drum of western arch.
Agia Barbara. Drum of western arch.
Agia Eufemia. Drum of western arch.
Agia Marina. Drum of western arch.
Agia Iuliane. Drum of western arch.

Πίνακας   5. *Οἱ Ἅγιες Εἰρήνη, Αἰκατερήνα, Βαρβάρα, ὁλόσωμες. Οἱ Ἅγιες Εὐφημία, Μαρίνα, Ἰουλιανή, σέ κύκλους. Ψηφιδωτό. Τύμπανο ΒΔ τόξου. Νάρθηκας.*

Die hlg. Irene. Westbogenfeld.
Die hlg. Katerina.
Die hlg. Barbara.
Die hlg. Euphimia.
Die hlg. Marina.
Die hlg. Juliane.

Anástasis (Resurrection), or the Descension to Hades. Drum of eastern arch.

Πίνακας 7. Ἡ Ἀνάσταση τοῦ Χριστοῦ (ἤ, ἡ εἰς Ἅδου Κάθοδος). Τύμπανο ΝΑ τόξου. Ψηφιδωτό. Νάρθηκας.

Die Auferstehung (Christi Hoellenfahrt).
Ostbogenfeld.

A(gios) Thomás.
Eastern part of southern arch.
A(gios) Barzolomeos.
In the middle of the same arch.
A(gios) Filipos.
Western part of the same arch.
Closed door. (The incredulity of Thomas.)
Niche in southern wall.

Πίνακας   8.   Τῶν θυρῶν κεκλεισμένων. (Ἡ Ψηλάφηση ἤ ἡ Ἀπιστία τοῦ
Θωμᾶ). Κόγχη νότιου τοίχου. Ὁ Ἅγιος Θωμᾶς (ὁλόσωμος ἀριστερά), ὁ Ἅγιος Βαρθολομαῖος (σέ κύκλο στό μέσο) καί ὁ Ἅ-
γιος Φίλιππος (ὁλόσωμος δεξιά). Ἐσωράχιο νότιου τόξου. Ψηφιδωτό. Νάρθηκας.

Der hlg. Thomas. Ostschénkel des Suedbogens.
Der hlg. Bartholomäus. Mitte des selb. Bogens.
Der hlg. Philipp. Westschenkel des selb. Bogens.
Durch verschlossene Tueren
Wundberuehrung, Ungläubigkeit des hlg.
Thomas Nische der Suedwand.

Agia Cekla.
Drum of western arch.
Saints Constantine and Helen.
Drum of western arch.
Agia Agaci.
Drum of western arch.
Agia An(a)stasia. Drum of western arch.
Agia Febronia.
Drum of western arch.
Agia Eugenia.
Drum of western arch.

Πίνακας 9. Ἡ Ἁγία Θέκλα (σέ κύκλο), οἱ Ἅγιοι Κωνσταντῖνος καί Ἑλένη (ὁλόσωμοι), ἡ Ἁγία Ἀγάθη (σέ κύκλο). Κάτω οἱ Ἅγιες Ἀναστασία, Φεβρωνία καί Εὐγενία (σέ κύκλο). Τύμπανο ΝΔ τόξου. Ψηφιδωτό. Νάρθηκας.

Die hlg. Thekla. Westbogenfeld.
Die hlg. Konstantin und Helene. Westbogenfeld.
Die hlg. Agathe. Westbogenfeld.
Die hlg. Anastasia. Westbogenfeld.
Die hlg. Phevronia. Westbogenfeld.
Die hlg. Eugenie. Westbogenfeld.

Agios Pimiɲ. Cross vault.
A(gios) Io(annis) the Kalivitis. Cross vault.
Agios Abramios. Cross vault.
A(gios) Io(annis) the Kolovós. Cross vault.
A(gios) Nikon the Metanoite.
Western wall.
A(gios) Makarios the Egyptien.
Northern arch.
A(gios) Io(annis) the one from the Climax.
Northern arch.
Agios Stéfanos, the Young.
Drum of aperture of three arches.
Agios Martinianós.
Drum of aperture of three arches
Agios Sabas. Eastern arch.
Agios Pajomios. Eastern arch.
Agios Efcimios. Eastern arch.
Agios Ceodosios. Eastern arch.

Πίνακας 10. Κάτω, ὁ Ἅγιος Νίκων ὁ Μετανοεῖτε. Στὸ σταυροθόλιο, σὲ κύκλους οἱ Ἅγιοι, Ποιμήν, Ἰωάννης ὁ Κολοβός, Ἀβράμιος καί
Ἰωάννης ὁ Καλυβίτης. Στὸ ἐσωράχιο τοῦ δεξιοῦ τόξου οἱ Ἅ-
γιοι, Μακάριος ὁ Αἰγύπτιος καὶ Ἰωάννης ὁ τῆς Κλήμακος. Στὸ
ἐσωράχιο τοῦ ἐπάνω τόξου οἱ Ἅγιοι, Σάβας, Παχώμιος, Εὐθύ-
μιος καὶ Θεοδόσιος. Στὸ ἀριστερό τύμπανο, σὲ κύκλους, οἱ Ἅ-
γιοι, Στέφανος ὁ Νέος καὶ Μαρτινιανός. Ψηφιδωτό. ΝΔ σταυροθόλιο τοῦ κυρίως ναοῦ.

Der hlg. Hirte. Kreuzgewoelbe.
Der hlg. Johannes, der Kalivitis. Kreuzgewoelbe.
Der hlg. Avramios. Kreuzgewoelbe.
Der hlg. Johannes, Kolovos.
Der hlg. Nikon Metanoite. Westwand.
Der hlg. Makarios der Egypter. Nordbogen.
Der hlg. Johannes der tis Klimakos.
Nordbogen.
Der hlg. Stephan o Neos. Bogenfeld ueber
dreifluegl. Oeffnung.
Der hlg. Martinianos. Bogenfeld ueber dreifluegl.
Oeffnung.
Der hlg. Savas. Ostbogen.
Der hlg. Pachomios. Ostbogen.
Der hlg. Evthymios. Ostbogen.
Der hlg. Theodosios. Ostbogen.

Martyr, bust on cross vault.
Martyr, bust on cross vault.
Martyr, bust on cross vault.
Martyr, bust on cross vault.
Model of church.
Southern window with two arches.
Agios Dimitrios. Northern wall.
Agios Sergios. Northern wall.
Agios Nikitas. Northern wall.
Agios Bacos. Northern wall.
Agios Nestor. In front of Saint Dimitrios.
Agios Ignatios. Below Saint Dimitrios.
Cross and blessing hand. Eastern vault.

Πίνακας 11. Οἱ Ἅγιοι Δημήτριος καί Νέστορ, στό ἐσωράχιο τοῦ τόξου. Τέσσερες Μάρτυρες σέ κύκλους, στό σταυροθόλιο. Τοιχογραφία. ΝΔ παρεκκλήσιο.

Maertyrer. Medaillon am Kreuzgewoelbe.
Maertyrer. Medaillon am Kreuzgewoelbe.
Maertyrer. Medaillon am Kreuzgewoelbe.
Maertyrer. Medaillon am Kreuzgewoelbe.
Abbild einer Kirche.
Ueber zweifluegl. Fenster.
Der hlg. Dimitrios. Noerdl. Bogenschenkel.
Der hlg. Sergios. Nordwand.
Der hlg. Nikitas. Nordwand.
Der hlg. Wakchos. Nordwand.
Der hlg. Nestor.
Dem hlg. Dimitrios gegenueber.
Der hlg. Ignazios.
Unter hlg. Dimitrios gegenueber.
Kreuz und segnende Hand. Ostwoelbung.

Virgin and Child. Niche.
Agios Azanasios. North from the Virgin.

Πίνακας 12. Ἡ Παναγία μέ τό Χριστό. Τοιχογραφία. Κόγχη τοῦ ΝΔ παρεκκλησίου.

Die Muttergottes mit Christus. Nische.
Die hlg. Athanasios. Noerdl. der Muttergottes.

Walking Christ. Eastern wall. Epigraph.
Agios Ioannis Prodromos. Epigraph.
Northern wall.

Πίνακας 13. Ὁ Ἰησοῦς Χριστός πηγαίνει νά βαπτιστεῖ. Ἐπιγραφή: ΑΦΕC
ΑΡΤΙ ΟΥΤΩ ΓΑΡ ΠΡΕΠΟΝ ΕΣΤΗΝ ΠΛΗΡΩΣΑΙ ΠΑ-
ΣΑΝ ΔΙΚΕΟΣΥΝΗΝ. Τοιχογραφία. Ἀνατολικός τοῖχος
ΝΔ παρεκκλησίου.

Christus schreitet zur Taufe. Inschrift-Ostwand.
Der hlg. Johannes der Vorläufer.
Inschrift-Nordwand.

A(gios) Lukás the Gurnikiotis. Western wall.
A(gios) Daniel. Southern arch.
A(gios) Ceodoros the Studitis.
Agios Ceoktistos. Cross vault.
Agios Doroceos. Cross vault.
Agios Nilos. Cross vault.
Agios Máximos. Cross vault.
Agios Ioanikios.
Drum of the three northern arches.
Agios Sisois.
Drum of the three northern arches.
Agios Hilarion. Eastern arch.
Agios Arsenios. Eastern arch.
Agios Efraim. Eastern arch.
Agios Antonios. Eastern arch.

Πίνακας 14. Κάτω, ὁ Ἅγιος Λουκᾶς, ὁ Γουρνηκηώτης. Στό σταυροθόλιο,
σέ κύκλους, οἱ Ἅγιοι, Θεόκτιστος, Μάξημος, Νεῖλος, Δωρό-
θεος. Στό ἐσωράχιο τοῦ τόξου, ἀριστερά, οἱ Ἅγιοι, Δανιήλ ὁ
τῆς Σκήτεος, Θεόδωρος ὁ Στουδίτης. Στό ἐσωράχιο τοῦ ἐπάνω
τόξου οἱ Ἅγιοι, Ἱλαρίων, Ἀρσένιος, Ἐφραίμ, Ἀντώνιος. Στό
τύμπανο, δεξιά, σέ κύκλους, οἱ Ἅγιοι, Ἰωαννίκιος καί Σισώης.
Ψηφιδωτό. ΒΔ σταυροθόλιο τοῦ κυρίως ναοῦ.

Der hlg. Lukas o Gournikiotis. Westwand.
Der hlg. Daniel o tis Skiteos. Suedbogen.
Der hlg. Theodoros o Stouditis. Suedbogen.
Der hlg. Theoktistos. Kreuzgewoelbe.
Der hlg. Dorotheos. Kreuzgewoelbe.
Der hlg. Neilos. Kreuzgewoelbe.
Der hlg. Maximos. Kreuzgewoelbe.
Der hlg. Joannikios. Bogenfld. des noerdl.
dreiflg. Fensters.
Der hlg. Sisois. Bogenfld. des noerdl. dreiflg.
Fensters.
Der hlg. Ilarion. Ostbogen.
Der hlg. Arsenios. Ostbogen.
Der hlg. Ephraim. Ostbogen.
Der hlg. Antonios. Ostbogen.

The five Saints.

Πίνακας 15. Δύο Ἅγιοι.
Τοιχογραφία. Νότιος τοῖχος ΒΔ παρεκκλησίου.

Fuenf Heilige.

The Pantocrator, the Virgin, the Prodromos,
four Archangels and 16 Prophets.

Der Pantokrator, die Muttergottes, Johannes
d. Vorläufer, 4 Erzengel und 16 Propheten.

Agios Vasilios. Niche of Northern wall.

Πίνακας 17. Ὁ Ἅγιος Βασίλειος. Ψηφιδωτό. Κόγχη βόρειου τοίχου, κάτω
ἀπό τό τροῦλλο.

Die Verkuendigung.
Nordwstl. Halbtrch. (zerstoert).
Der hlg. Basilios.
Nische der Nordwand.

The Nativity. Mosaic.

Πίνακας 18. Ή Γέννηση τοῦ Χριστοῦ. Ψηφιδωτό. ΝΑ ἡμιχώνιο, κάτω ἀπό τόν τροῦλλο.

Christi Geburt. Mosaik.

*A(gios) Io(annis) or Jri(sosto)mos. Niche of
Southern wall below the Nativity. Mosaic.*

*Πίνακας 19. Ὁ Ἅγιος Ἰωάννης ὁ Χρυσόστομος. Ψηφιδωτό. Κόγχη νότιου
τοίχου, κάτω ἀπό τή Γέννηση.*

*Der hlg. Johannes o Chrysostomos.
Nische der Suedwd. unter der Geburt. Mosaik.*

The Baptism.

Πίνακας 21. Ἡ Βάπτιση. Ψηφιδωτό.
ΒΔ ἡμιχώνιο, κάτω ἀπό τό τροῦλλο.

Die Taufe.

I(isus) X(ristós). Christ.
Archangel Uriel.
Agios Zajarias.
Archangel Raphael.
Agios Kleopas. Northern aperture of three arches.
Agios Ananias. Northern aperture of three arches.
The Panagia (Virgin). On the eastern wall.
Agios Panteleimon. On the western wall.
Agios Sosípatros. On the southern window.
Agios Iason. On the southern window.

Πίνακας 22. Ὁ Ἰησοῦς Χριστός, ὁ Ἀρχάγγελος Οὐριήλ, ὁ Ἅγιος Ζαχαρίας
καί ὁ Ἀρχάγγελος Ραφαήλ, στό σταυροθόλιο, σέ κύκλους. Ἡ
Παναγία Δεξιοκρατοῦσα, κάτω ἀπό τό Χριστό. Οἱ Ἅγιοι
Κλεώπας καί Ἀνανίας σέ κύκλους, ἀριστερά. Οἱ Ἅγιοι Σωσί-
πατρος καί Ἰάσων σέ κύλους, δεξιά. (Ὁ Ἅγιος Παντελεήμων,
κάτω ἀπό τόν Ἅγιο Ζαχαρία, δέν φαίνεται). Ψηφιδωτό. Σταυροθόλιο νότιας θύρας.

Jesus Christus. Medaillon.
Der Erzengel Ouriil. Medaillon.
Der hlg. Zacharias. Medaillon.
Der Erzengel Raphael. Medaillon.
Der hlg. Kleopas. Medll. noedl. dreifluegl.
Oeffnung.
Der hlg. Ananias. Medll. noedl. dreifluegl.
Oeffnung.
Die Muttergottes. Rechtshaltend. An der Ostwand.
Der hlg. Panteleimon. An der Westwand.
Der hlg. Sosipatros. Am Suedfenster.
Der hlg. Jason. Am Suedfenster.

Agios Lukás. Mosaic. Western wall.

Πίνακας 23. Ὁ Ἅγιος Λουκᾶς. Ψηφιδωτό. Δυτικός τοῖχος σταυροθολίου, βόρειας θύρας.

Der hlg. Lukas. Mosaik Westwand.

I(isus) from Naví. Fresco.
Eastern wall below the Virgin.

Πίνακας 24. Ἰησοῦς ὁ τοῦ Ναυῆ. Τοιχογραφία. Ἀνατολικός τοῖχος σταυροθολίου, βόρειας θύρας.

Jesus o tou Navi (von Navi) Wandml.
Ostwand unter der Muttergtt.

Marble Iconostasis.
«Panton Elpís». Portable icon of the Virgin of
the Passion.
The «Pantocrator». Portable icon of Christ.

Πίνακας 25. Μαρμάρινο τέμπλο (εἰκονοστάσι). Δύο εἰκόνες: α΄ Παναγία Ἀ-
ριστεροκρατοῦσα «Ἡ Πάντων Ἐλπίς», στό τύπο τῶν εἰκόνων
τῆς Παναγίας τοῦ Πάθους. β΄ Ὁ Χριστός Παντοκράτωρ. Ἔργα
Μιχαήλ Δαμασκηνοῦ (16ος αἰ.).

Marmorikonostase.
«I Panton Elpis» (Die Aller Hoffnung).
Tragbare Ikone der Schmerzensmutter.
Der «Pantokrator». Tragbare Ikone Christi
Schmerzensmutter.

The «Platitera». Epigraph, mosaic. Niche.

Πίνακας 26. Ἡ Πλατυτέρα. Ἐπιγραφή: «Τῷ Οἴκῳ σου πρέπει ἁγίασμα Κύριε εἰς μακρότητα ἡμερῶν». Ψηφιδωτό. Τεταρτοσφαίριο ἀψίδας Ἱεροῦ.

Platytera (Muttergottes), Inschrift. Mosaik-Nische.

Marble plate on the floor.

Πίνακας 27. Μαρμαροθέτημα στό δάπεδο τοῦ Ἱεροῦ.

Fussbodenbelag aus Marmor.

Agios Dionisios Areopagitis. Mosaic.
Western arch.
Agios Hieroceos. Mosaic. Western arch.
Agios Grigorios Nisis. Mosaic. Western arch.
Agios Filoceos. Mosaic. Western arch.
Agios Antipas. Mosaic. Cross vault.
Agios Elfecerios. Mosaic. Cross vault.
Agios Ancimos. Mosaic. Cross vault.
Agios Policarpos. Mosaic.
Epigraph. Mosaic. Arch of niche.

Πίνακας 28. Οἱ Ἅγιοι, Ἀντίπας, Ἐλευθέριος, Ἄνθημος καί Πολύκαρπος σέ κύκλους στό σταυροθόλιο. Ἀριστερά ὁ Προφήτης Δανιήλ. Δεξιά οἱ Ἅγιοι Τρεῖς Παῖδες. Στό ἐσωράχιο τοῦ τόξου οἱ Ἅγιοι, Γρηγόριος ὁ Νύσης, Φιλόθεος Ἱερόθεος καί Διονύσιος Ἀρεοπαγίτης. Ψηφιδωτό. Διακονικό, δεξιά ἀπό τό Ἱερό.

Der hlg. Dionysios der Areopagit.
Mosaik. Westwand.
Der hlg. Jerotheos. Mosaik. Westl. Bogen.
Der hlg. Jerotheos.
Mosaik. Westl. Bogen.
Der hlg. Grigorios, o Nyssis.
Mosaik. Westl. Bogen.
Der hlg. Philotheos. Mosaik. Westl. Bogen.
Der hlg. Antypas. Mosaik. Kreuzgewoelbe.
Der hlg. Elevtherios. Mosaik. Kreuzgewoelbe.
Der hlg. Anthimos. Mosaik. Kreuzgewoelbe.
Der hlg. Polykarpos. Mosaik. Kreuzgewoelbe.
Inschrift. Mosaik. Bogennische.

Πίνακας 29. Ὁ Προφήτης Δανιήλ ἀνάμεσα στούς λέοντες. Ψηφιδωτό. Βόρειο τύμπανο σταυροθολίου Διακονικοῦ.

Hosioi. Left middle of the arch.

Πίνακας 30. Οἱ Ἡγούμενοι, **Φιλόθεος, Ἀθανάσιος, Θεοδόσιος** καί Μοναχοί. Τοιχογραφία. Δυτικό μισό τοῦ τόξου εἰσόδου. Κρύπτη.

Osioi. Linke Haelfte des Bogens.

Agios Anikitos.
Agios Arezas.
Agios Fotios.
Agios Vikentios.

Πίνακας 31. Οἱ Ἅγιοι, Ἀνήκητος, Ἀρέθας, Φώτιος καί Βικέντιος. Τοιχογραφία. Σταυροθόλιο ἀμέσως μετά τήν εἴσοδο. Κρύπτη.

Der hlg. Anikitos.
Der hlg. Arethas.
Der hlg. Photios.
Der hlg. Vizentios.

Closed door (The Incredulity of Thomas).
Southern wall.

Πίνακας 32. Τῶν Θυρῶν Κεκλεισμένων, (Ψηλάφηση ἤ Ἀπιστία τοῦ Θωμᾶ).
Τοιχογραφία. Νότιος τοῖχος τοῦ ΝΔ διαμερίσματος. Κρύπτη.

Ton Thyron kekleismenon (bei verschlossenen
Tueren). Die Ungläubigkeit des hlg. Thomas.
Suedwand.

The Crucifixion. Eastern wall.

Πίνακας 34. Ή Σταύρωση. Τοιχογραφία. Ἀνατολικός τοῖχος τοῦ ΒΑ διαμερίσματος. Κρύπτη.

Die Kreuzigung. Ostwand.

Apóstolos Lukás.
Apóstolos Markos.
Apóstolos Andreas.
Apóstolos Matceos.

Πίνακας 35. Οἱ Ἀπόστολοι Ἀνδρέας καί Μανθέος καί οἱ Εὐαγγελιστές Λουκᾶς καί Μάρκος. Τοιχογραφία. Σταυροθόλιο, νότια τοῦ προηγουμένου. Κρύπτη.

Der Apostel Lukas.
Der Apostel Markus.
Der Apostel Andreas.
Der Apostel Mantheos.

The Descension. Eastern wall.
The Burial and «Behold in the Tomb».
Southern wall.

Πίνακας 36. Ἡ Ἀποκαθήλωσῃ, ἀριστερά, μόλις διακρίνεται. Ὁ Ἐνταφια-
σμός τοῦ Χριστοῦ καί «Ἴδετε τόν Τάφον». Τοιχογραφία. ΝΑ
ρ̣ ̣ ̣ ̣ἴο διαμέρισμα. Κρύπτη.

Die Kreuzabnahme. Ostwand.
Die Grablegung. «Idete ton Taphon». Suedwd.

The Descension. Eastern wall.

Πίνακας 37. Ἡ Ἀποκαθήλωση. Τοιχογραφία. Ἀνατολικός τοῖχος τοῦ ΝΑ γωνιαίου διαμερίσματος. Κρύπτη.

Die Kreuzabnahme. Ostwand.

Marble Temple.
The Apóstolos (unknown). Cross vault.
The Apóstolos (unknown). Cross vault.
The Apóstolos (unknown). Cross vault.
The Apóstolos Filipos. Cross vault.

Πίνακας 38. Τό Ἱερό καί τό μαρμάρινο τέμπλο. Ὁ Νιπτήρας, ἀριστερά καί ὁ
Μυστικός Δεῖπνος, δεξιά. Τέσσερες Ἀπόστολοι στό σταυροθόλιο, σέ κύκλους. Τοιχογραφία. Ἱερό. Κρύπτη.

Marmortempel.
Der Apostel (unerkannt). Kreuzgewoelbe.
Der Apostel (unerkannt). Kreuzgewoelbe.
Der Apostel (unerkannt). Kreuzgewoelbe.
Der Apostel Philipp. Kreuzgewoelbe.

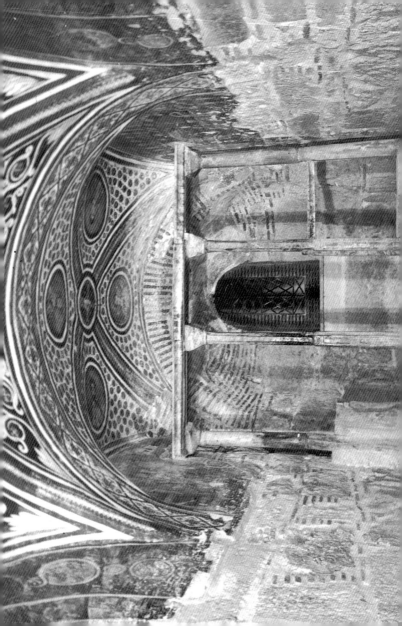

The Lord's Supper. Southern wall.

Πίνακας 39. Ὁ Μυστικός Δεῖπνος. Τοιχογραφία. Νότιος τοῖχος τοῦ Ἱεροῦ. Κρύπτη.

Das hlg. Abendmahl. Suedwand.

*The two temples from the Est : To the left the
Temple of Hosios Lukás, and to the right
the Church of the Virgin.*

*Πίνακας 40. Οἱ δύο ναοί ἀπό τά ἀνατολικά. Ἀριστερά ὁ ναός τοῦ Ὁσίου
Λουκᾶ (11ος αἰ.) καί δεξιά τῆς Παναγίας (10ος αἰ.).*

*Die beiden Kirchen von Osten. Links die Kirche
des hlg. Lukas und rechts die Muttergotteskirche
Bild am rueckwt. Umschlag (V).*